M E X

GOOD STORIES REVEAL as much, or more, about a locale as any map or guidebook. Whereabouts Press is dedicated to publishing books that will enlighten a traveler to the soul of a place. By bringing a country's stories to the English-speaking reader, we hope to convey its culture through literature. Books from Whereabouts Press are essential companions for the curious traveler, and for the person who appreciates how fine writing enhances one's experiences in the world.

"Coming newly into Spanish, I lacked two essentials—a childhood in the language, which I could never acquire, and a sense of its literature, which I could."

—Alastair Reid, *Whereabouts:*
Notes on Being a Foreigner

OTHER TRAVELER'S LITERARY COMPANIONS

Amsterdam edited by Manfred Wolf
Australia edited by Robert Ross
Chile edited by Katherine Silver
Costa Rica edited by Barbara Ras
with a foreword by Oscar Arias
Cuba edited by Ann Louise Bardach
Greece edited by Artemis Leontis
Israel edited by Michael Gluzman and Naomi Seidman
with a foreword by Robert Alter
Italy edited by and translated by Lawrence Venuti
Japan edited by Jeffrey Angles and Thomas Rimer
with a foreword by Donald Richie
Prague edited by Paul Wilson
Spain edited by Peter Bush and Lisa Dillman
Vietnam edited by John Balaban
and Nguyen Qui Duc

MEXICO

A TRAVELER'S LITERARY COMPANION

EDITED BY

C. M. MAYO

WHEREABOUTS PRESS
BERKELEY, CALIFORNIA

Published in the United States by
Whereabouts Press
Berkeley, California
www.whereaboutspress.com

Distributed to the trade by
Consortium Book Sales & Distribution

Map of Mexico by BookMatters

Manufactured in the United States of America

Library of Congress Cataloging-in-Publication Data

Mexico : a traveler's literary companion /
[compiled by] C. M. Mayo.
p. cm.—(Traveler's literary companion)
ISBN-13: 978-1-883513-15-3 (pbk. : alk. paper)
ISBN-10: 1-883513-15-4 (pbk. : alk. paper)
1. Short stories, Mexican—Translations into English.
2. Mexican fiction—20th century—Translations into English.
I. Mayo, C. M.   II. Series.
PQ7288.M49   2006
863'.0108972—dc22
2005034427

5 4 3 2 1

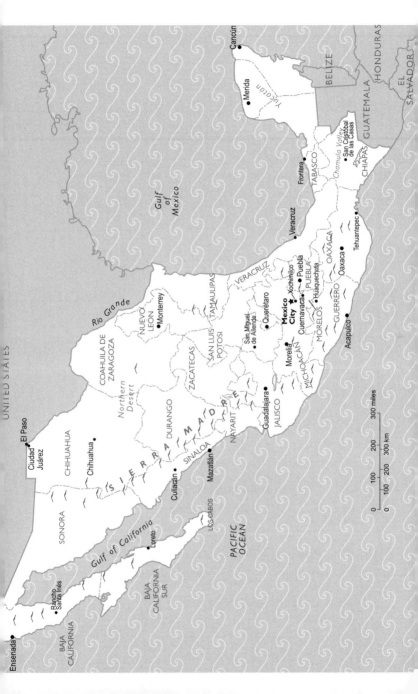

Contents

Map   v

Preface   ix

Acknowledgments   xiv

THE U.S.–MEXICO BORDER

—{ Tecate }—

Daniel Reveles   *Big Caca's Revenge*   1

—{ Ciudad Juárez }—

Carlos Fuentes   *Malintzin of the Maquilas*   21

THE NORTH

—{ In the State of Sinaloa }—

Inés Arredondo   *The Silent Words*   30

—{ In the State of Chihuahua }—

Jesús Gardea   *According to Evaristo*   38

—{ The Northern Desert }—

Ricardo Elizondo Elizondo   *The Green Bottle*   54

—{ Baja California }—

Agustín Cadena   *Lady of the Seas*   78

C. M. Mayo   *Rancho Santa Inés: Fast!*   86

CENTRAL MEXICO

—{ Mexico City }—

Carlos Monsiváis   *Identity Hour or,
What Photos Would You Take of the Endless City?*   92

Juan Villoro   *One-Way Street*   101

Guadalupe Loaeza   *Oh, Polanco!*   107

Fernando del Paso   *The Emperor in Miravalle*   112

—{ Near Cuernavaca, Morelos }—

Mónica Lavín   *Day and Night*   116

—{ In the State of Puebla }—

Pedro Ángel Palou   *Huaquechula*   125

Ángeles Mastretta   *Aunt Elena*   136

—{ Morelia, Michoacán }—

Raúl Mejía   *Banquets*   144

—{ Guadalajara, Jalisco }—

Martha Cerda   *And One Wednesday*   160

—{ Querétaro (in the Bajío) }—

Araceli Ardón   *It Is Nothing of Mine*   168

ALONG THE GULF OF MEXICO

—{ In the State of Tabasco }—

Bruno Estañol   *Fata Morgana*   177

—{ In the State of Veracruz }—

Ilan Stavans   *Twins*   184

Raymundo Hernández-Gil   *Tarantula*   191

SOUTH AND SOUTHWEST

—{ Acapulco }—

Julieta Campos   *She Has Reddish Hair
and Her Name Is Sabina*   207

—{ Isthmus of Tehuantepec, Oaxaca }—

Alberto Ruy Sánchez   *Vigil in Tehuantepec*   210

—{ Chiapas }—

Rosario Castellanos   *Tenebrae Service*   224

YUCATÁN

Laura Esquivel   *Swift as Desire*   235

Permissions   239

Preface

Since its independence from Spain in the early nineteenth century, Mexico has been, variously, empire, republic, and dictatorship, its once far-flung boundaries brutally cut back by the United States and the secession of what is now Central America. Thus modern-day Mexico's curious shape: a thick, curling torso (the mainland) with one dangling, withered arm (Baja California) and the other a muscle curled into a fist (Yucatán). Historian Timothy E. Anna writes, "Mexico was, and still is today, a country defined by its regions." Could any be more different than Baja California's searing deserts and Yucatán's lush jungles? (Or, for that matter, Yucatán and anyplace else?)

"Mexico" means the land of the Mexica, that tribe of destiny better known as the Aztecs. At the time of the Conquest in the early sixteenth century, the Mexica were the dominant, though certainly not the only indigenous people within the territory that is today the Republic of Mexico. Later, during colonial times, people took to identifying themselves by their province or region—New Spain or New Galicia or California, for example—or by their ethnic group. There were, as there are today, Creoles (those of purely Spanish ancestry), as well as Tarascans living on the mirror-like lakes of Michoacán, Tzotzils in Chiapas, and Triquis in the highlands of Oaxaca, to give only a few of innumerable examples. The national myth propagated by the state in the wake of the early twentieth-century revolution is that to be Mexican is to belong to *la raza cósmica*, the Cosmic Race of the mestizo, born of the Spanish father and Indian mother. True, the overwhelming majority of modern Mexicans are mestizos; however, this overlooks not only Mexico's many indigenous peoples but also the hundreds of thousands of Mexicans descended from Africans, Basques, Chinese, Lebanese, Jews, Germans, French, Italians, Irish, English, and others.

That said, Mexican literature— a vast banquet— is one of the greatest achievements of the Americas. And yet we who read in English go hungry, for so astonishingly little of it has been translated. This is more astonishing still when one considers that the United States shares a two-thousand-mile-long border with Mexico.

We have, however, been allowed to sample some of the most enticing flavors. Mexican literature begins with the poems, myths, chronicles, and prophecies of its indigenous peoples. In English we have, for example, Miguel León-Portilla and Earl Shorris's sweeping anthology *In the Language of Kings*, which includes the Nahua chronicle "The Fall of Tenochtitlan," the haunting poems of Nezahualcoyotl, and the sixteenth-century *Popol Vuh*, sometimes called the Mayan Bible. We also have English translations of Spanish works about the Conquest, most notably Bernal Díaz del Castillo's sublime and epic memoir *The True History of the Conquest of Mexico*. From the colonial period we have the searing "intellectual autobiography" of the nun and literary prodigy Sor Juana Inés de la Cruz, translated by Margaret Sayers Peden as *A Woman of Genius*. Of the work of twentieth-century writers, we have more translations, including the fiction of Juan Rulfo and Carlos Fuentes, and the poetry and prose of Nobel Prize–winner Octavio Paz. I would be remiss not to also mention Laura Esquivel's charming *Like Water for Chocolate*, a best-seller in English and Spanish, which was made into a popular movie. On the downside and in spite of a number of books of Mexican literature in translation and shorter works in magazines such as *The Paris Review, Tameme, Terra Incognita,* and *Two Lines,* most of the vast array of Mexican literature remains untranslated. All the more reason, dear reader, why the book you now hold in your hands is a rare treat, for it also offers a taste of the sharply different and pungent flavors of Mexico's regions.

My main criteria for selection were literary quality and a specific sense of place and/or regional culture. I focused on contemporary writing, which I defined as short stories, novel excerpts, and creative nonfiction published after 1973—though I made an exception to this last guideline for Rosario Castellanos, a native of Chiapas and one of Mexico's greatest writers. Despite a rich tradition of writing in English about Mexico, I stayed away from English-language writing, with two exceptions: an excerpt from my own memoir *Miraculous Air*, which recounts an interview with a rancher who had worked on Baja California's Transpeninsular Highway, and "Big Caca's Revenge" by Chicano writer Daniel Reveles, set in the border city of Tecate. In sum, my definition of "contemporary literary Mexican writing" is, to a degree, an arbitrary slice that is mushy about the edges, as are all definitions of convenience.

Overall, I aimed to achieve diversity not only of places, but also of styles and sensibilities—no small task, for "literary" writing in Mexico is dominated by a Mexico City elite. Culturally, demographically, economically, intellectually, and politically, Mexico City has no equivalent in the United States. You might think of it as Washington D.C., Los Angeles, Boston, and New York City rolled into one. Most anthologies of Mexican literary writing tend toward a Mexico City–dominated "Who's Who"—as does this one, if to a much lesser degree, for indisputably much of the best writing is being produced in the capital.

I did as most anthologists do: I read, I read some more, I asked advice, I read—a seemingly endless cycle that yielded treasures, among them, Pedro Ángel Palou's "Huaquechula," set in the state of Puebla, and Mónica Lavín's "Day and Night," set in the village of Acapatzingo in the state of Morelos. In addition, however, I made a "Call for Submissions" that I emailed to hundreds of writers, translators, and professors. Many forwarded it—I know it ended up on several web sites, including that of the American Literary Translators Association. I also snail-mailed 650 flyers with the same to translation and Spanish departments in universities throughout the United States, Mexico, Canada, the U.K., and even to a few in Australia. What arrived in my mailbox was—as I had hoped—a big, juicy stack of envelopes. Araceli Ardón, a writer from Querétaro, sent her not-yet-published "It Is Nothing of Mine." From Geoff Hargreaves I received his translation of the brilliant and devastating "The Green Bottle" by

Monterrey's Ricardo Elizondo Elizondo—another writer new to me. Translator Harry Morales sent Alberto Ruy Sánchez's memoir, "Vigil in Tehuantepec" and Ilan Stavans's "Twins," about two small-town Lebanese brothers. From Philip Garrison I received his translation of Michoacán writer Raúl Mejía's (very spicy) "Banquets." From Provo, Utah, came Daryl R. Hague's translation of the eerie "Tarantula" by state of Veracruz native Raymundo Hernández-Gil, a writer whose work had only been published in Spanish in a Brigham Young University student magazine—a venue far below the radar of Mexico City's literati, indeed.

Throughout Mexico there are so very many writers whose work has yet to be translated, or, though translated, deserves a far wider readership in English. Given the scope and extent of this anthology, a number of pieces did not fit for reasons quite other than their quality. (What to do with something set in Paris? Arizona? outer space?) I aimed for a certain balance—no banquet should be all savory, or all sweet.

As they say in Mexico, *buen provecho!*

C. M. Mayo

ACKNOWLEDGMENTS

Sincere thanks to David Peattie, visionary publisher of Whereabouts Press, who invited me to do this anthology and who has been a great supporter all the way through. A very special *gracias* to my Mexican husband, Agustín Carstens, who listened to me read many of these stories in Spanish, gave me his advice, and patiently answered my many questions about the translations. Thanks to the Virginia Center for the Creative Arts, where I spent part of a residency preparing this anthology. Thanks also to Katherine Silver for her careful copyediting and advice, and to William C. Gruben, Robert Jackson, David Lida, Victoria Ludwin, Alice Jean Mansell, Patricia Mazón, Margaret Sayers Peden, José Antonio Ramírez, Cecilia Ramos, Barbara Ras, Mark Schafer, José Skinner, and all the many writers and translators who sent work for me to consider (would that this anthology could have been longer!). And finally, thanks to the writers and the translators gathered here, without whom there would be no book, no banquet.

For Agustín, *como siempre*

Big Caca's Revenge
Daniel Reveles

A NUMBER OF YEARS have passed since the events that follow took place. And yet, the scar remains. We had a terrorist lurking in Tecate. Time has failed to erase the memory. You can still hear the locals talking about *el terrorista* with residual fear coloring their voices. In the cantinas, the cafés, in the plaza. Sometimes, while waiting for the light to turn red to get safely across our only avenue, I can hear little snatches of conversation, and the dreaded name is whispered, a name that can still send goosey chills down all twenty-four vertebrae of the spinal column—Big Caca.

Big Caca is as despicable a man as ever broke tortilla and

DANIEL REVELES was born in Los Angeles of Mexican-born parents. Since his youth he has been involved in some aspect of the entertainment industry, as a disc jockey, recording artist, songwriter, and television producer. He fell in love with the magical pueblo of Tecate twenty-five years ago and has remained there ever since, living and writing in the company of coyotes on à ranch on the outskirts of town. His books of short stories are *Enchiladas, Rice, and Beans* (1994), *Salsa and Chips* (1997), and *Tequila, Lemon, and Salt* (2005).

is despised with a passion. This dreaded individual is the commander at the border. He alone decides what can come into Mexico from the U.S. and what cannot. He is not awash with the milk of human kindness and no one has ever seen a rainbow round his shoulder. One day when golden sunbeams fell on Tecate and all was right with the world, I came through the border in my usual high spirits. Someone once said, I forget who, power corrupts and absolute power corrupts absolutely. Meet Señor Absolute Power. Big Caca writes legislation as needed and sets importation fees on the spot. He found a six-pack of petunias I picked up at Garden Town Nursery in San Diego and immediately threatened to confiscate my car. The petunias cost me a buck. But I got to keep my car.

In pursuit of Truth I'm obliged to tell you that he was never officially baptized Big Caca by the local padre. His real name was Ismael Cacabelos. He was built low to the ground. What I believe is called the center of gravity was buried in that massive gluteal region we call *nalgas*. The fit of his olive green uniform was a disgrace to his office, but the .45 on his hip swelled the brass buttons on his bosom with pride and importance. He weighed more than a small car. But inside that enormous exterior, we knew there was a tyrant trying to get out. When you looked into his face you would logically conclude that you were looking at an eggplant with a mustache and a wart on the left nostril. In short, Big Caca was a frontal assault on the optic nerve.

The man himself seemed unaware of his physical disadvantage. He considered himself a ladies' man and was perennially in pursuit of that endeavor. This may have been due to some undiagnosed mental disorder. He often trolled the plaza for candidates and one day saw a woman of extra-ordinary beauty he'd never seen before. She was slim where slimness was preferred and bountiful where bountiful was desirable. She was dressed in shimmering turquoise pants and matching jacket that fitted her like the skin on a mango. Big Caca held his breath and missed a heartbeat. He inquired as to her identity and learned her name was Lizette. Lizette became an obsession.

It is said in town that he made daily prayers and lit candles in hopes the beautiful Lizette would one day come through the gate, something like a black widow who waits for a victim to get tangled in its web. But his supplications to divine deities were not answered. It had been weeks since his first sighting of the apparition in the plaza. He was on the edge of abandoning hope. Then one ripe summer day Doña Fortuna, as Fate so often does, delivered that something into his web.

Big Caca stood at the border extorting fees in the name of the law, as usual. It was a slow day. It was nearly two in the afternoon and nothing much was coming through. A pickup truck with a used washing machine came in and that was good for twenty American dollars, but he could tell it was going to be a dismal day. He looked up at the next car in line. A white Volkswagen. Not much there, he thought, when he saw the woman at the wheel. Lizette!

Lizette was returning from a day of heavy shopping at the wholesale showrooms in the garment district in San Diego. She did this often. But not for herself. She shopped for her clients, ladies who didn't have time or didn't have the proper papers to cross the border. It was a business. A highly profitable business. She always brought back several hundred dollars' worth of women's apparel and never paid bribe or duty. She made it a point to cross the border late at night when the sleepy officer would be sipping coffee in the little guardhouse watching the late-night show, and he would just wave her through. If she just had the right connection, she thought, she could enter Mexico with most of Macy's inventory and not get fleeced. But she didn't have the right connection and when she saw the eggplant with all the brass buttons and the glimmering badge of authority she knew she was going to get hit pretty hard. She always did her best to avoid him but she knew who he was.

"*Buenas tardes*, señorita," he oozed. "What do you have to declare?"

"*Buenas tardes*, Comandante," she answered melodically in metrical cadence, as though reciting a lyric poem. "Only a few items of clothing for my personal use."

Big Caca walked officiously around to the other door and began to grope through the contraband. He found dresses, skirts, and blouses. Upon further snooping he found at least twenty pairs of panties in a variety of colors and bras to match. He held up a shimmering black Playtex underwire bra designed to separate and lift, then the matching black panties no larger than a cocktail napkin.

"And all this is for your personal use, señorita?"

"A girl never has enough underwear, you know."

"What you have here, señorita, comes close to seven hundred dollars in duty."

Any other girl would have thought all was lost. But not our beautiful Lizette. She took the bra he was fondling and held it up to herself. "What if I just keep this one?" Before he could find words she reached in the bag and withdrew a Playtex "Barely There" creation in ripe plum with front closure. "Or this? Which one do you think looks best on me?" She watched the eyes in the eggplant swell to the size of ping-pong balls. "I'd like to keep the matching *calzones* you presently hold in your hand. I can return the rest. Would that be all right?"

Big Caca ogled the bra she was holding to her bosom and fingered the slinky garment in his hand. "Look, señorita, we are here to control the borders of our sovereign nation, not to discommode nice people. Why don't you meet me for a drink at La Fonda this evening? Seven, say?"

Lizette found that important connection she needed to stay in business. "Seven it is," she sang, and the Volkswagen rumbled into Mexico.

Now, the story circulating around Tecate has several versions. We must accept the fact that a small portion of this drama is pure conjecture as there were no witnesses. But I will identify these passages in the interest of honest reporting.

The affair between the Comandante and Lizette was both romantic and symmetrical. Big Caca got to play *nalgas*, and Lizette could drive into Mexico with an armed missile if she so desired. As promised, the following scenes are conjecture because only the two of them were present when they happened.

One pleasant day in June Big Caca invited Lizette for a weekend in the country. They crossed the border into the U.S. early in the morning and were soon in Temecula, a picturesque wine-growing village in San Diego county. It is bucolic and quiet, claims the most spectacular sunsets in the county, and produces some fine wines that win high praise from those who know good wine when it rolls on the discerning tongue.

The happy couple registered at the Chardonnay Inn, a bed and breakfast in a pretty garden setting not far from the vineyards. Big Caca was more interested in the first B than the second, but he agreed with Lizette that a walk along a quiet lane was the ideal way to say adios to the day. He was dressed in a pair of baggy cotton pants and a Mexican *guayabera* blouse. He felt naked without his uniform, the gleaming emblem of authority on his breast, and the .45 to back it up. But those articles of his authority had to stay in Mexico. Lizette was in ratty blue jeans and shirt. But in all probability her underwear was exquisite. They both wore sandals.

"I always think of the sunset as the sun's final farewell before slain by the night. It is as sad as it is beautiful," Lizette recited in a romantic whisper.

Big Caca was not a poet. The red sunset reminded him of *huevos rancheros*. He garbled something in his throat and Lizette took this to mean that he was too overcome with emotion to express his innermost thoughts about the sunset. They joined hands and stood among the grapevines until the last light expired. Big Caca could feel the effects of the Viagra he'd taken earlier and was looking forward to nightfall and the B.

A red and blue light flashed behind them. Big Caca thought maybe it was part of the celestial phenomena at sundown. It wasn't. It was a white station wagon with a cage in the back. The U.S. Border Patrol.

The grim-looking officer in forest green uniform stood eight-two at the very least and didn't give the impression he was the type who cared much for natural spectacles in the heavens. He swaggered up to Big Caca.

"Citizenship," he demanded. It wasn't a question. Big Caca reached for his wallet while the Border Patrol reached for his pistol but didn't draw. Seeing everything was legal he gave the papers back. "Okay, Hosay, no *problema*." Big Caca bristled at the disrespect.

"Now, yours," he said looking at Lizette.

"My purse is back at the inn!"

"Sure it is. You won't be picking grapes tomorrow, señorita. Come along and take a ride with me. I'll get you back to your own country and we won't have no problems."

Big Caca nearly exploded. A few miles south of where he now stood, and just across a four-strand barbed wire fence, he had the authority to make mincemeat out of this big stupid *cabrón* and he was being taken for a common grape picker! He began to protest in badly frayed English.

"You just stay right there, Hosay," the Jolly Green Giant said in a voice Big Caca recognized as dangerous.

Big Caca quickly realized he was outside his sphere of power. If he challenged the officer he would most likely radio for a back-up and haul his *nalgas* away, too. He swallowed his humiliation in livid silence.

"Don't be upset, *mi amor*. Condemn the law, not its agent," Lizette said in her sweet poetic voice. "He is only performing his duty."

Big Caca stood and watched impotently as his beautiful Lizette was put in the cage and driven away like a rabid dog.

"Duty!" he spat as the wagon disappeared. "I'll show you duty!"

Big Caca was no philosopher, and, as we saw earlier, he did not have the heart of a poet. He watched the Border Patrol disappear over the crest of the road and the burning fire of vengeance was already smoldering in his bowels.

The foregoing scene ends the portion of surmise I alluded to earlier. Now we can proceed to the area of reality. We have reliable witnesses for everything that follows.

Big Caca's revenge began the very next day.

We were standing at the bar of the Diana, a saloon named in honor of the famous huntress whose portrait dominates the back bar. The deity of the hunt was watching us from her position. She must have left all her clothes somewhere in the forest for she was stark naked, back arched, muscles tense, as she prepared to release an arrow from her oaken bow. Mario, the bartender, was practicing his alchemy with tequila and limes in the blender. There was the banker, two lawyers, and Jerry, an American who owned a big factory that employed a hundred workers. And there was Chavez, the dentist, who hopefully had no appointments this afternoon. It was a friendly group of regulars. We all had gotten to know each other over a period of many years. A trio consisting of guitar, accordion, and bass viol provided jumpy little tunes that added to the conviviality.

The sudden dimming of the bright daylight from outside announced that an addition to our party had just entered through the door. There was a total eclipse. We all turned toward the door as one to see who had come to raise a glass with us, and the place fell silent as Moctezuma's tomb. Laughter froze in the air. All conversation stopped. The guitar and the accordion and the bass viol produced no sound. Diana held back the arrow and gave us the same look she must have given Actaeon when she sicced his own hounds on him and they turned him into taco meat. It looked like one of those freeze-frames you see in the movies.

Big Caca stood in the doorway.

He didn't speak to any of us although he knew everyone there by name and would often allow us to buy him drinks until he dropped. He didn't even say *buenas tardes* or *hola* to the room in general. He marched directly to Jerry.

"Hi, Comandante," Jerry said genially. "What'll you have? I buy!"

We all knew this was Big Caca's favorite transitive verb so we remained bereft of speech when he answered.

"May I see your documents that allow you to remain in Mexico?"

Jerry could not believe the words. None of the rest of us could either. We thought he was having a joke. There are probably forty or fifty Americans living or working in Tecate. They came in search of a simpler, gentler lifestyle, or maybe they just wanted a little magic in their souls. They found it here in Tecate and stayed. They had all their official paperwork done when they first came to Mexico. But after ten or twenty years nobody bothered to carry them or keep them up to date. "Not on me, Comandante, back at the office." As he said this Jerry knew if he still had the forms filed away somewhere in his office they would be dated twelve years ago. Big Caca knew it, too.

There can be little doubt that Big Caca was replaying that scene featuring the big ugly Border Patrol officer who called him Hosay and interrupted his tryst with Lizette.

"You have no documents? Foreigners are required by law to carry them at all times. I think you'd better come with me."

"But Comandante, you've known me for years. I can't just leave the factory to run by itself for the rest of the day." We all heard a nervous panic in Jerry's voice.

"I am sorry. We cannot make a piñata of the law."

When he escorted Jerry out of the Diana we knew it wasn't a joke. We all ran to the door to see what was going to happen. We watched in horror as Big Caca said, "It is my duty to deport you back to the United States." He put him in his official military vehicle and pulled away from the curb. When he got to the border he followed the same standard procedure U.S. Border Patrol agents follow with undocumented Mexicans. He escorted Jerry to the gate and watched him enter the United States.

And that was just the beginning of Big Caca's revenge.

Not more than a couple of days later Mildred Harris was just leaving Mini-Mercado Perez with two bags of groceries. She was a sweet grandmother type, dressed in what was once known as a housedress, blue gingham covered with daisies. Grandma Millie bought them through Dr. Leonard's catalogue where she also bought her toe separators and her husband's incontinence pants. Mimi at La Princesa Salon on Calle Hidalgo kept Mildred's iron gray hair lustrous and nicely arranged. The sweet old woman's eyes were blue, bright, and intelligent.

"*Buenos dias*, señora."

Grandma Millie looked up at the sound of the familiar voice and broke into a broad smile when she recognized the comandante. They had met eight years earlier when she and Fred first came to live here after his retirement and saw each other often around town. "Oh, *buenos dias*, Comandante! How nice to see you!"

"And you," the comandante answered.

"I've been doing some shopping," she said breathlessly. "We'll have the grandchildren over for the weekend." Grandma was nearly dancing with delight at having her grandchildren. The shopping bags were filled with all the things she wouldn't give her own children when they were little: potato chips, chocolate wafers, Fritos, and tortilla chips. "They eat everything in sight, you know. But then, isn't that what grandchildren are for? They are to spoil rotten!" She bobbed her head and laughed. "It will be nice to hear the voices of children at play. What brings you out here, Comandante?"

Big Caca wasn't laughing, nor did he join Millie on the subject of the joys of hearing the voices of grandchildren in the house. He despised children. And he wasn't smiling, either.

"Señora, do you have your documents of legal residency in Mexico?"

Millie still didn't get the big picture. "Why, no. I suppose they might be back at the house. Fred would know where they are. He saves everything. He's a regular pack rat, I swear. Would you believe Fred still has all the AARP magazines since—"

Big Caca didn't show a great deal of interest in AARP or what Fred packed away. "You do not have your documents, señora?"

There was panic in Millie's voice for the first time in the conversation. "No, I do not."

"Then, you'd better come with me."

"Go with you! Where?"

"Back to the United States. It is the law that all foreign residents must have proper papers on them at all times." He opened the passenger side of his vehicle and assisted with her bags of potato chips and chocolate wafers and the rest of the junk food intended for spoiling her grandchildren.

The little grandma was now genuinely frightened. "But you just can't pick me up off the street and throw me out of the country. Fred's at home waiting for me. He'll think I was in an accident. He'll worry about me!" Tears rolled out of her blue eyes.

Big Caca looked at the frightened grandmother, and thought, I'm sure the U.S. Border Patrol listens sympathetically when they pick up some poor Mexican woman on her way home to her children after a day of cleaning houses.

"We cannot make a piñata of the law, señora." He drove her to the border and sent her through the gate. The last thing he saw was an American customs officer going through her shopping bags.

Every morning Big Caca sprang from bed to the sound of drums and bugles calling him to duty. Like a ferret he searched the little town for an illegal American resident then deported him (or her) back to the U.S. He nailed Fred leaving El Gordo's Licores with a six-pack of Corona. Harry Jones, with whom he used to toss back a tequila now and again, was in the optometrist's waiting room without proper documents. This town hasn't seen anything yet, he gloated, I'm just getting started!

By now, of course, the news was running through Tecate

like a SARS epidemic. Americans kept a low profile and were getting harder to find walking down the street. Today Big Caca decided he would just slip over to the Parque Industrial and see if he could catch Norman in the office of his cigar box factory. To borrow your American expression, Big Caca was on a roll!

The guard at the gate felt little ice crystals form in his bloodstream when Big Caca pulled up. "*Buenas dias*, Comandante," the guard said with a little tremolo in the voice. "Visiting us today?"

"Yes," the comandante answered and drove through.

He marched into the lobby and barked, "I am here to see Norman Miller."

The pretty dark-eyed receptionist turned the color of an uncooked tortilla. "I'm so sorry, Señor Miller is not in today."

And she wasn't lying. Norman Miller escaped out the back door and was now in the alley hiding behind a dumpster along with a purebred garbage hound looking for a late breakfast.

Big Caca was well aware most of the Americans were living here on their social security checks. They drove late model cars. They lived in nice places, ate good food, and employed a maid. In their own country they would be living below the poverty line. Here in Mexico they used the city parks, enjoyed the security of safe streets and a fire department. And they paid no taxes! Big Caca felt justified. He was performing his duty for his country and solving the illegal alien problem in Tecate at the same time. He had a thirst for revenge. It became a Holy Crusade.

Big Caca glanced at his watch. Eleven in the morning.

He lusted for one more hit before taco time. From his heart of oak the sap began to flow into his veins, delivering new energy and virility to his tissues. His skin tingled. In minutes he was in a state of complete arousal. He was horny for gringos! Big Caca knew his next stop. If he went to Los Encinos right now he could round up a whole bunch of illegal aliens playing soccer or shuffleboard or some such nonsense. A surprise raid. Yes!

Los Encinos is a vast park with a couple of soccer fields, horseshoe and shuffleboard courts, and a baseball diamond surrounded by a forest of immense oak trees. Big Caca parked at a safe distance and adjusted the focus of his high-powered field glasses. He could see at least four gringos. He watched the action.

"Way to go, Manuelito!" Manuelito smacked one out to left field where there was no one in attendance and cruised in to second base.

"*Ándale*, Charlie, breeng heem home. *Sí!*" Charlie swung and missed.

There were close to ten men on the baseball diamond, hardly enough to form two teams, but the old men were having a great time pitching, hitting, and running bases.

Keeping to the darkest shadows cast by the giant trees, step by careful step, Big Caca drew closer. Inch by inch he slithered like a serpent. When he thought he was within reasonable range he broke into a dead run toward the middle of the field. Now, it must be understood that a dead run for a man of his tonnage could never be said to be swift as an arrow from Diana's bow.

"*La migra! La migra!*" someone yelled.

The Americans scrambled into the woods like Mexican

farmworkers abandoning the lettuce fields in Bakersfield when the Border Patrol shows up.

Within the first week Big Caca's rampage had a profound effect on our peaceful little pueblo and the Cafeteros called an emergency session at La Fonda to deal with the crisis. Present at the long table were the banker, the lawyer, our poet/accountant, El Ranchero, the doctor, two local merchants, and myself. The waiter placed three coffee pots on the table.

"Señores. It is time for action. The situation in our pueblo is *intolerable!*" the banker announced. "Road construction is at a standstill because El Weelie who maintains our graders and Caterpillars is hiding under his house. Father Ruben is hiding El Smeety in the church basement, and he's the technician who services the electronics in our factories!"

Our poet/accountant came out of his chair, nearly spilling his coffee. "We will not leave here until we have a viable solution. Suggestions, señores."

El Ranchero was first to rear up. "Assassination!"

"I can prepare a lethal injection," our good doctor offered.

One of the merchants leaped to his feet. "Look, this problem should go to the highest authority in Tecate, our Presidente Municipal. Certainly he can put a stop to it."

"You forget," the lawyer was quick to say, "that our esteemed Presidente is employed by the municipality. Big Caca represents the federal government. El Presidente is powerless under the law."

"There is only one avenue open to us, gentlemen," our poet/accountant intoned. He waited until he was sure he had everyone's undivided attention. Then he gave us his mind in one word that left this august body of coffee drinkers speechless, which has never been known to happen. "*Brujeria!*"

"*Sí*, witchcraft!" someone shouted. I didn't see who. "*Sí! Doña Lala could turn him into a toad just like that!*" The speaker snapped his fingers to illustrate his point.

"He already *is* a toad!"

"A potion!" someone else suggested. "Babalu could prepare a potion."

"A curse!" El Ranchero cried, tipping his chair over backward as he stood.

The idea of witchcraft was gaining strength. "That is the answer," our poet/accountant agreed. "I will go myself to Babalu and have her prepare a curse."

"What kind of a curse?"

"Something that would make his ears fall off!"

"I had something else in mind."

"I have it, señores, I have it!" We all looked over to the speaker. El Tacón, proprietor of the biggest shoe store in Tecate, came to the vertical position. "Catch a pompous ass with another pompous ass!" We waited for El Tacón to elucidate. "Bring Big Nalgas Machado over here and our problem is solved within the hour!"

"A cop? Just what do you have in mind?" the banker asked.

"Get Machado over here and I'll explain in detail."

"Where is he?" someone asked.

The lawyer answered. "I saw him earlier directing traffic at the intersection of Avenida Juárez and Cárdenas. The traffic light is not working properly. It gives a green light to both streets at the same time. He's probably still there."

"If he hasn't been flattened!" El Ranchero added.

"Get him over here at once!" the banker ordered.

I could see no possible solution to the crisis. If our Presidente was powerless, what could one fat local cop do against a federal comandante? I was dying to know the plan so I volunteered to go fetch Machado.

If you've been following the story and not nodding off during the high drama, you know that Big Caca didn't have a romantic gene in his corpulent body. His heart was not a sunny garden where love and kindness bloom in profusion. The garden of his heart was choked with weeds. Life was about women, power, and rank.

He was at this very moment on his way to Lizette, who was waiting for him in her Olga "Sensuous Solutions" push-up bra and Gloria Vanderbilt panties. El Comandante had three hundred *caballos* galloping between the shafts of his 1992 Ford LTD. He held the rank of *comandante federal de aduana*, and more power than any living soul in Tecate! And the Viagra was already delivering an ample supply of blood where it was needed. Milton might have said Big Caca was throned on highest bliss. He pressed down on the accelerator.

Big Caca glanced in his rearview mirror and saw a series of red and blue lights flashing merrily. Sometimes the Viagra produced this symptom. But these lights were coming from the rooftop of a black sedan of the type issued by the municipality to its police officers. What on earth! he grumbled. Probably a stupid new policeman who has yet to be trained to recognize the immunity of the all-powerful comandante. On second examination he recognized the big, brown smiling face of Big Nalgas Machado. It wouldn't be the first time Machado had used this means to stop and have a chat or to invite him to his ranch for a *carne asada*. He pulled over.

"Machado! How are you, *cabrón*? Haven't seen you for a while, *qué onda*?"

"*Buenas tardes*, Comandante. Can I see your driver's license?"

He's having his little joke, the comandante thought. I'll have mine. "You mean you don't recognize me, *cabrón*? You'd better get fitted for glasses!"

"Your license, please, Comandante."

The comandante lost his patience. "Are you crazy, Machado? You've known me for eighteen years."

"Just following procedure, Comandante."

Big Caca didn't want to waste any more time. The extra blood supply was already doing its work in the designated area and Lizette was waiting. He produced the document. "There, *cabrón*!"

Machado looked at the license. "Perfectly valid, issued by the state of Baja California Norte."

"Satisfied?"

"Yes, Comandante, your license is in order. But you're driving a car with American plates."

"So what?"

"It is against the law for anyone with a Mexican driver's license to drive a car with American plates."

Big Caca was well aware of the law but he also knew the law did not apply to him. "You've seen me drive this car since I bought it. Where's the problem?"

"I have to confiscate the car."

"Confiscate the car! You're crazy!"

"If you will just step out, Comandante, I will radio for a tow truck."

"A tow truck! Are you insane Machado? Can you see who I am?" Flames leaped from his eyes, steam spewed from his ears like the twin smokestacks at the Tecate Brewery.

They argued heatedly for a brief interval and in a few minutes a tow truck from El Tigre Towing Service pulled into the scene with rotating amber lights and backed up to the comandante's car.

For the first time in his long career of power and abuse, Big Caca groveled. "Come on, Machado, I'll treat you to a shooter of José Cuervo and a slice of lemon. I know you can overlook this minor infraction."

"I'm sorry, Comandante." Big Nalgas wasn't, but it sounded sincere. He may have been thinking of the day he and his wife were returning from Home Depot with a microwave. *Now you know, Machado, that it is unlawful for a microwave to come in to Mexico.* It cost him fifty American. The silver-gray LTD with three hundred horses between the shafts was hauled away by the *nalgas* like a dead horse.

"You will be sorry, *cabrón!*" Big Caca lost his composure. "You do this and you'll live to regret it!"

"We cannot make a piñata of the law."

The pandemonium in the Diana the next day reached the critical stage. Another decibel added to the chaos and the narrow saloon would have exploded. It was bedlam set to music except that the guitar and the accordion and the bass viol could only be heard in those brief intervals required to put glass to lips and take a sip. Mario was mixing drinks as fast as his hands could grasp the neck of a bottle. Diana seemed pleased to see us in festive celebration. She smiled down at us from the back bar, quite unconcerned for her nakedness. A bunch of us locals and nearly all the Americans came out of hiding to celebrate the end of the reign of terror. The Cafeteros immediately declared this date a national holiday, and sent the bill to the Presidente for his signature. Like most of their legislation, the bill never passed. We were packed in like jalapeños in a jar. Jerry was there, and Grandma Millie's husband, Fred, and Charlie, who was up at bat when they got busted. In less than an hour Tecate's fattest cop became a national hero. Everybody wanted to embrace him and fill his glass.

It's been well over ten years since these events occurred and Big Nalgas Machado hasn't paid for a drink since.

—{ Ciudad Juárez }—

Malintzin of the Maquilas

Carlos Fuentes

For Enrique Cortázar, Pedro Garay, and Carlos Salas-Porras

HER PARENTS gave Marina that name because of their desire to see the ocean. When she was baptized, they said, maybe this one will get a chance to see the ocean. In the clump of shacks in the northern desert, the young would get together with their elders, and the elders would tell how, when they were young, they wondered what the ocean was like. None of us had ever seen the ocean.

Now, as the frozen January sun rises, Marina sees only

CARLOS FUENTES (1928–) was born in Panama of Mexican parents. The son of an ambassador, Fuentes spent his childhood in Latin America and Washington D.C. Widely considered Mexico's leading writer, he is the author of more than twenty books, including the novels *Aura* (1986), *The Death of Artemio Cruz* (1991), *The Old Gringo* (1985), and *The Crystal Frontier* (1997), a novel in nine stories from which this excerpt is taken. In 1987 he was awarded the Cervantes Prize, the highest honor given to a Spanish-language writer. He divides his time between Mexico City and London.

the thin waters of the Río Grande, and the sun feels that everything's so cold it would like to slip back down between the dun sheets of the desert from which it is beginning to emerge.

It's five o'clock and she has to be at the factory by seven. She's late. What made her late was making love with Rolando last night, going with him to El Paso, Texas, on the other side of the river, and returning late, alone, shivering as she crossed the international bridge to her one-room house with lavatory in Colonia Bellavista, Ciudad Juárez.

Rolando had stayed flat on his back in bed, one arm folded behind his head, the other flattening a cellular phone to his ear. He looked at Marina with weary satisfaction, and she didn't ask him to take her home. She could see how comfortable he was, so boyish, all cuddled up, and also so open, so moist and warm. Above all, she saw him ready to start working, making calls on his cellular phone since very early—the early bird catches the worm, especially if the bird's a Mexican making deals on both sides of the border.

She glanced at herself in the mirror before leaving. She was a sleepy beauty, with the thick eyelashes of a young girl. Sighing, she put on her blue down jacket, which looked bad with her miniskirt because it hung to her knees while the skirt just reached her thighs. She stuffed her work sneakers into her bag and slung it over her shoulder. Unlike the gringas, who walked to work in Keds and put on their high heels in the office, Marina always wore pointy high heels to work even if they sank into the mud from time to time. Marina wouldn't sacrifice her elegant shoes for anything: no one would ever see her in worn-out shoes looking like some Apache.

She caught the first bus on Cadmio Street, and, as she did every other morning, she tried to look beyond the dirt-colored neighborhood, the shacks that looked as though they'd popped up out of the ground. Every day, without fail, she tried to look at the vast horizon. The sky and the sun seemed her protectors; they were the beauty of the world, they belonged to everyone and cost nothing. How could ordinary people make something as beautiful as that? Everything else was ugly by comparison. The sun, the sky . . . and—so they said—the sea!

She always ended up looking toward the gullies that tumbled down toward the river, as if her eyes were pulled by the law of gravity, as if even within her soul all things were always falling down. Even at this early hour the Juárez gullies looked like anthills. Activity in the poorest neighborhoods began early, as swarms of people poured out of the shacks down by the edge of the narrow river, trying to cross. She turned away, uncertain if what she saw annoyed her, embarrassed her, aroused her sympathy, or made her feel like imitating those crossing to the other side.

Better she fix her eyes on a solitary cypress tree until she couldn't see it anymore.

Instead of the cypress, Marina saw only concrete, wall upon wall of concrete, a long avenue boxed in by concrete. The bus stopped at a field where some boys in shorts were playing soccer to keep warm, and then, shivering, it crossed the vacant lot to the next stop.

She sat down next to her friend Dinorah, who was wearing a red sweater, blue jeans, and loafers. Marina held on tight to her bag but crossed her legs so Dinorah and the other passengers could see her classy high heels with a chain instead of a leather strap across the ankle.

They made their usual small talk: How's the little one, who'd you leave him with? At first, Marina's questions irritated Dinorah and she would pretend to be distracted—looking for a piece of chewing gum in her bag or fixing her mop of short orange-colored curls. Then she'd realized she'd be running into Marina on the bus every day of her life and she would quickly answer, My neighbor's going to take him to a day-care center.

"There's so few of them," Marina would say.

"Of what?"

"Day-care centers."

"Around here, sister, there's not enough of anything for anything."

She wasn't about to tell Dinorah to get married, because the one time she did, Dinorah had responded angrily, Why don't you go ahead and do it first? Set an example, Miss Know-It-All. Marina wasn't about to point out that, though neither of them was married, she didn't have a child—that was the difference. Didn't the kid need a father?

"What for? Around here, men don't work. You want me to support two instead of just one?"

Marina told her that with a man at home she'd be able to defend herself better against the pests at the factory, who were always after her because they saw that she was defenseless, that no one stood up for her. Marina's comment infuriated Dinorah, and she told Marina she was sick and tired of her, God may have thrown them together on the same bus, but if Marina went on giving advice no one asked for, she'd quit talking to her. Marina should stop being such a hypocrite.

"I've got Rolando," said Marina, and Dinorah almost died laughing: All the girls have Rolando, and Rolando has all the girls. Who do you think you are, you idiot? Marina began to sob, though the tears didn't roll down her cheeks but instead welled up in her eyelashes, and Dinorah felt bad. She pulled a tissue from her pocket, hugged Marina, and wiped her eyes.

"You don't need to worry about me, honey," said Dinorah. "I know how to protect myself from the boys in the factory. And if someone tells me I've got to fuck him to get a promotion, I'll just change factories. Anyway, nobody moves up around here. We just go sideways, like crabs."

Marina asked Dinorah if she changed jobs a lot. Marina's job was her first, but she'd heard that when the girls got fed up with one place they moved on to another. Dinorah told her that after you've done the same work for nine months your sides start to hurt and your back won't let you sleep.

They had to get off to change buses.

"You're late too."

"I guess it's for the same reason you are," Dinorah said with a smile. They walked off laughing, arms around each other's waists.

The plaza, crowded with little shops and all kinds of stalls, was already bustling. Everyone was exhaling winter mist, and vendors were showing off their merchandise or hanging up their signs: Hurry, hurry, get your beans from

Jean. The two women stopped to buy corn, delicious ears of it dripping melted butter and still steaming. They giggled at an advertisement: Use Macho Man for Sexual Deficiency. Dinorah asked Marina if she'd ever met a man with sexual deficiency. Marina said no, but that didn't matter as much as choosing the right man. The right man? Well, the one you really like. Dinorah said that the men with sexual deficiencies were almost always the braggarts, the ones who bothered them and tried to take advantage of them in the factories.

"Rolando's not like that. He's very macho."

"So you told me. And what else does he have?"

"A cellular phone."

"Wow." Dinorah rolled her eyes mockingly but said nothing more because the bus arrived and they got on to make the last leg of the trip to the assembly plant. A very thin but good-looking young woman, with an aquiline beauty unusual in those parts, came running up to catch the bus. She was in a Carmelite habit and sandals. As she took the seat in front of them, Dinorah asked if her little feet weren't cold like that in winter, without stockings or anything. She blew her nose and said it was a vow that only made sense in the frost, not in the summer—she used the English word.

"Do you two know each other?" asked Dinorah.

"Only by sight," said Marina.

"This is Rosa Lupe. You can't recognize her when she's in a saintly mood. But believe me, she's normally very different. Why'd you get involved with this vow business?"

"Because of my *famullo*."

She told them she'd been working in the plants for four

years but her husband—her *famullo*—still hadn't found work. The children were the reason: who would take care of them? Rosa Lupe looked at Dinorah, although not with obvious malice. The *famullo* stayed home with the kids, at least until they were grown.

"You support him?" asked Dinorah, to get back at Rosa Lupe for her remark.

"Just ask around at the factory. Half the women working there are the breadwinners in their families. We're what they call heads of households. But I have a *famullo*. At least I'm not a single mother."

To avoid a fight, Marina commented that they were coming into the nice area, and without saying another word the three of them looked at the rows of cypresses lining both sides of the road. They were waiting for the incredibly beautiful vision that never failed to dazzle them though they'd seen it countless times. The television assembly plant, a mirage of glass of glass and shining steel, like a bubble of crystalline air. It was almost like a fantasy to work there, surrounded by purity, by brilliance, in a factory so clean and modern, what the managers called an industrial park.

It was one of the plants that allowed the gringos to assemble toys, textiles, motors, furniture, computers, and television sets from parts made in the United States, put together in Mexico at a tenth the labor cost, and sent back across the border to the U.S. market with a value-added tax. About such things the women knew little. Ciudad Juárez was simply the place where the jobs called them, jobs that did not exist in the desert and mountain villages, jobs that were impossible to find in Oaxaca or Chiapas or in the capital itself. Those jobs were here, and even if the salary was a tenth what it was in the United States, it was ten times more than the nothing paid everywhere else in Mexico.

At least that was what Candelaria wore herself out telling them. A woman of thirty, Candelaria was more square than fat, the same size on all four sides. She always wore traditional peasant clothing, though it was difficult to tell from which region of Mexico, as the totally sincere, serious, but smiling Candelaria mixed a little bit of everything: pigtails tied with Huichol wool, Yucatán-style smocks, Texan skirts, Tzotzil belts, huaraches with Goodrich tire soles available at any market. And since she was the lover of an antigovernment union leader, she knew what she was talking about. It was a miracle she hadn't been blackballed from all the assembly plants. But Candelaria always managed to save her skin: she was a wizard at changing jobs. Every six months she went to another factory, and each time, her boss breathed a sigh of relief because the agitator was leaving, and as far as the owners were concerned, frequent job changes meant little or no change in political consciousness: there wasn't enough time to stir anyone up. Candelaria would just shake her comical pigtails and go on raising consciousness in one place after another, every six months.

She had been working in the plants for fifteen of her thirty years and didn't want to ruin her health. She'd already worked in a paint factory and the solvents had made her sick—imagine, she said at the time, spending nine months filling paint cans just to end up painted inside. That's when she met Beltrán Herrera, a mature man—

which is why Candelaria liked him—mature but with tender eyes and vigorous hands; dark-skinned, he had graying hair and wore a moustache and glasses.

Candelaria, Bernal said to her, they wouldn't give you water around here if you were dying of thirst. Whatever you need you've got to earn with the sweat of your brow. They talk about costs and profits, sure, but there's no insurance for work-related accidents, no medical treatment, no pension, no compensation for marriage, maternity, or death. They're doing us a big favor giving us work, thank you very much, so keep your mouth shut. Say so much as three little words, my dear Candelaria, "three little words," as the old song goes, strike by coalition, strike by coalition, strike by coalition—say it three times like a litany, Candy sweetest, and you'll see how they turn pale, promise you raises and bonuses, respect your opinions, urge you to switch factories. Do it, darling. I'd rather you switched than died.

"This place is so beautiful," sighed Marina, taking care not to let her stiletto heels puncture the green lawn marked with the double warning NO PISE EL PASTO / KEEP OFF THE GRASS.

"It looks like Disneyland," said Dinorah, half joking, half serious.

"Sure, but it's full of ogres who eat innocent princesses like you," said Candelaria with a sarcastic smile, fully aware that her irony was lost on these three.

Translated by Alfred Mac Adam

The Silent Words

Inés Arredondo

For José de la Colina

NAMES. They also enter the realm of mystery, they correspond to other things. That's how it was with Eduwiges. He couldn't settle for calling her Eluviques so he called her simply Lu, and lu is the name of a halftone on the Chinese musical scale: precisely the meaning and the sound that vibrated in him when he saw her move, with her tall, elastic young body over the tender, dark greens of his parcel of land, when he heard her laugh with her ringing laughter that set the birds fluttering.

INÉS ARREDONDO (1928–89) was one of Mexico's most distinguished short story writers. She grew up in Culiacán, in the northwest state of Sinoloa. Many of her stories are set in the early twentieth century in or near the great house of Eldorado, her family's sugarcane hacienda; however, she spent her adult life, with the exception of two years in Uruguay, in Mexico City. She died suddenly of a heart attack in 1989. A collection of her stories, *Underground River and Other Stories*, was published in English in 1996.

She asked him once: "If you know so many things, why don't we go away to the city? I know you have money saved up, but you're a tightwad. There are rich Chinese there, very rich, living in the lap of luxury. Open a store in Culiacán. I'll help you."

"Why do I live on the jade-green hill?
I laugh and don't respond. My serene heart:
a peach blossom carried off by the current.
Not the world of men,
I live under another sky, in another land."

"Go to hell. You and your foolishness."

But she had given him three children and had sung under the thatched roof.

Then there was that other business, too, the fact that Don Hernán, every once in a while, would speak seriously with him and, when he was in a good mood, would call him Confucius or Li Po. Don Hernán had traveled all over the world, read everything. And later, when the great persecution of the Chinese in the Northwest came, he hadn't allowed any of them to be touched, neither rich nor poor. And he had loaned him, surely on a whim, that book translated from the English, and Manuel had copied down the poems with such difficulty, because when it came to reading, he could read easily, but writing, he never had written since he had first learned how. Who was he going to write to? He wouldn't even have anyone to write to in Chinese, although he could have remembered enough characters to do it. "No more yearning to return / forgetting everything one has learned, among the trees." That's what he had decided when he arrived, how many years ago now? For that he has no memory. Yes, he does remember his teacher over there. The silence. . . .

"Manuel, I'm expecting visitors tomorrow. I want you to bring me some more poppies, but they have to be the very prettiest ones you have."

"Yes, yes." And he moves his head as if it were sitting there unattached atop his long, smooth neck.

"My parents-in-law are coming, you know. Well, the people who are going to be my parents-in-law. They're coming to ask for my hand."

"OK, OK, I give you flowells."

"Thank you, Manuel. Oh! By the way, I'm going to invite you to the wedding."

"Good, very good."

He, too, had gotten married and Don Hernán himself had been his best man. Maybe that's why Don Hernán had felt obliged, when Lu went away with Ruperto, to send for him and tell him that they could make her come back, put her in jail, take her children away, they could . . . they could do so many things. . . . Don Hernán was angry.

No. He had always sold produce to Ruperto and he was an honorable man. Lu had given him happiness and three children. On those afternoons when Ruperto would go out with his truck, and they would carry the vegetables between the two of them, after they were finished, Lu would come up and offer them fresh fruit juice, as he had taught her to do, and it wasn't their fault if they knew how to laugh loudly at the same time, and to talk the same, with the same pronunciation, about the same things, standing there for a long time; he had seen it while he listened quietly. That went on for years. As for the children, those little untamed beasts . . . they were identical to her, even physically molded in her image. They had her big yellow eyes, although they were slightly slanted; furthermore, he had made every effort to teach them what he had learned when he was a child, as small as they, and they had only responded with indications of surprise. Astonishment, if not repudiation, is what he had felt in each of them when, at the right moment, he had taken them to see the San Lorenzo after the flood, majestic and calm, and in a low voice, playing with a leaf or caressing a stone, he had said slowly, "Far away, the river runs into the sky."

Despite his warnings, in the course of their games they trampled and destroyed the nursery beds, and he hadn't managed to get them lovingly to transplant a single little plant or to stand still for an instant, quietly watching something, for instance the moon, so strange and intimate.

It wasn't even people's names, the names of things, that escaped him, it was only their articulation. And that was all: enough for them to consider him inferior, everyone, everyone; at times, not even Don Hernán understood him fully, deeply. Only the other Chinese. Yes, it was not a coincidence that he didn't talk like the others, that he had his own special way of doing it.

"Old ghosts, new ones
Worry, crying, no one.
Aged, broken,
I sing only for myself."

The clarity was beginning. Emerging from silence, it

remains quiet for a while and touches things imperceptibly. Quietly.

It was the best time to dig his bare, shriveled foot into the spongy earth to feel, in the darkness, the first damp lettuce, which he didn't see but remembered from the day before, from so many days before when he already knew when it would be ripe; in order to cut it, noiselessly, with the sharp knife. And to stay here like this, relishing the silence of that thing that wasn't work but prophecy and knowledge. Then, stealthily, the light began to appear, until the birds awoke. "A rooster crows. Bells and drums on the river bank. One cry follows another. A hundred birds all at once."

He kept walking on his knees between the furrows, refining the words inside himself; there was no reason to stop. Meanwhile, he felt on his face, on his back, on his tranquil sides, how the deep breathing was beginning in the orchards surrounding his parcel. Forever dark and secret, closed in on themselves, the enormous orchards were beginning to stir. When the light had become too vivid, it was enough to lift his head a bit for his eyes to rest on the dark stain projected by the trees.

It was not time to cultivate, it was time to sell. Going into the bamboo-and-straw hut, forever cool under the great mango tree left in the middle of his tilled land, he eats something for breakfast and gets ready. He doesn't realize, maybe because no one, no one pointed it out to him, that he dresses the same as he did in his country, that the enormous, cone-shaped hat woven with his own hands isn't like the ones worn by the men in town, except, of course, for the other men of his race that live there. Careful to keep

his balance, he lifts the two, very large, baskets, arranges
the twine, adjusts them at either end of the long pole that
he places across his shoulders, and lifts the weight as if he
didn't feel it. He trots evenly along the edge of the canal
crossing the orchard, then straight down the dusty path
stretched among the fruit trees. He passes the big house
and waves to the people strolling in the gardens, through
the yards, without losing the rhythm of his little bird-hops.

From the time he reaches the first houses, without raising his voice too much, he begins to announce his wares.

"Vegetal, vegetal."

He knows it's *vegetables* but he can't pronounce it. There
are so many things he'd like to say, he's tried to say, but he
gave up because they sound ridiculous, they sound ridiculous to him in his stammering of a child that doesn't know
how to talk yet. Only Don Hernán. . . . But with the others he doesn't insist; he understands that if you don't make
yourself understood, other people think it useless to
respond, to talk to you, because they feel you don't understand, that your inability to express yourself correctly is a
sure sign of your incapacity truly to understand. He didn't
feel rancor or get upset; he had known from childhood: "If
we don't know the value of men's words, we don't know
them." And he is a man, even though he's old, even though
the inexplicable clumsiness of the roof of his mouth, of his
tongue, forces him to resign himself to the simplest of
interactions, and other people don't see him as he really is.
They're fond of him, it's true; they ask him to do them
favors and they do favors for him; but they don't talk to him
like they do among themselves, even though some of them
are so stupid.

"Manuel! Do you have any squash?"

"Manuel!"

How long has that been his name? How many years has he been in this town? How long ago was he born? There inside him, deep down, is his real name, but he hasn't told it to anyone. Not even secretly to Lu, whispering in her ear, many years ago.

He quickly finishes selling his produce and goes back to work.

Out back is the poppy bed. Beautiful to behold like no other. He thinks about the Englishman, about De Quincey, whose words he has copied, who never saw them in their winged splendor, filling the air with their fragile charm. It's February; in March he'll have to work at his private harvest of opium, but it isn't really work: it brings him pleasure, intense pleasure. While he prunes the plants, he watches them and listens to the sighs of unopened petals. He cuts a bud.

"I'm not ashamed, at my age, to put a flower in my hair.

The one ashamed is the flower crowning an old man's head."

In March, he harvested the double poppies, triple poppies, that people bought eagerly. But he saved the reserves and began distilling the thick juice from the heart of the flowers.

Every year he did this, and he secretly saved it for moonlit nights, lonely nights, or when he was going to converse, deliberately, with his own people.

In May, when the sun dazzles you, makes you sweat, but

still doesn't weigh you down or put you to sleep, they arrived.

His three children and a stranger, in Ruperto's strong, modern truck:

"These young people are here to claim their inheritance, their right to your land . . ."

He didn't hear any more. He didn't want to hear more.

He looked at his tall, wild, alien children.

He knew that the land belonged to Don Hernán, who had given it to him to cultivate, so there would be vegetables, flowers in town, and that Don Hernán wasn't going to let anyone take a single dirt clod of this land away from him. But that wasn't the issue.

He waited until nightfall. Slowly, he began smoking his long pipe. There was no hurry. When he figured he was near paradise, he set fire to his bamboo hut, lay back down in bed, and kept on smoking.

Translated by Cynthia Steele

According to Evaristo
Jesús Gardea

THE YEARS HAVE NOT WORN AWAY my memory of Evaristo. By now he is mingling with the dust, the sun forever on his eyes. Today he rises in my own eyes. He descends gently to my soul, as if seeking the half-light below the eaves. He hasn't changed a bit. It's true: he's the same man as always. He is accompanied by the perfume of profound emptiness; it issues from all over his slim body at the slightest movement. When he speaks, it accompanies his words and gestures like wind from hidden waters.

JESÚS GARDEA (1939–2000) was born in Ciudad Delicias, Chihuahua. He lived most of his life in Ciudad Juárez, where he both practiced and taught dentistry. With no formal training in literature, he began writing in his late twenties and, in 1979, published his first collection of short stories. A year later, Gardea's second collection of stories, *Septiembre y los otros días*, received the prestigious Xavier Villaurrutia Prize. He wrote six collections of short stories, twelve novels, and one collection of poems, *Songs for a Single String* (2002). *Stripping Away the Sorrows from This World,* a collection of Gardea's short stories, translated by Mark Schafer, was published in 1998.

My father was his friend. He met and grew to know him in another town when Evaristo was a young herbalist. My father met him at his place of business, behind a tiny drawer that held the sales receipts; Evaristo sat there all day, from morning to the final hours of the afternoon. He didn't even leave the drawer to go eat. Around noontime, his wife would leave the store to bring him lunch in a pan from a restaurant. The herbalist devoured the meal and then resumed his silence after a conclusive belch.

My father never knew quite how he managed to draw words from the man's mouth and become friends with him.

The woman was twice his age. Secluded amid the aromas of the various herbs, she kept a sharp eye on him, observing him from where she sat at the back of the store. She would only get up to attend to customers, go to the restaurant, and gather up the day's earnings and close the shop. The first time my father began to converse with the herbalist, the woman was agitated and could not keep still, even though she kept watching him attentively. My father had only seen her a couple of times in his life and he didn't like her. She was extraordinarily thin, sallow, lacking any shine, and taller than her husband. After closing the shop, the couple would walk to the nearby plaza. They never looked at each other. They preferred to contemplate the kiosk and the children playing there. They would stay until dusk, then follow the road back to their house.

When my father first came to that town, seven years had passed since the two had gotten married, since the man had become a cashier, an herbalist. At the very beginning, in the days after the wedding, the town had showered the young husband with sympathy while condemning the woman's appetite. This is what they told my father. But he found only indifference, as if the townspeople were blind and deaf to them.

With a sprig of herbs—dispensed by the woman at the back of the shop—in his left hand, my father stood before the herbalist, extending his right hand in greeting, open as the sun:

"Onésimo Sanjurjo!" he said.

Evaristo, who had extended his hand to receive payment, was suddenly disconcerted. But then, quickly rotating his hand, he offered it for shaking.

It was still several hours before the afternoon would turn to dusk. My father and his new friend talked the whole time without pause like long-lost friends. My father was resting the hand that held the sprig on the counter, close to the money drawer, and its fragrance delighted him; it placed on his tongue the intense light of summer itself.

"Go figure, Sanjurjo," said Evaristo, "the true nature of things. They have no borders. This is the first time I've really smelled peppermint, now that you're sticking it under my nose."

"I call it mint, Evaristo," my father responded, and held the sprig up to his eyes and shook it like a rattle. The aroma spread all through the air then headed out to die on the deserted beach of the street. My father enjoyed producing those little waves. He assured us that he heard them crashing and then saw them breaking up into a green, translucent foam. But his friend finally put a stop to it:

"Sanjurjo, please stop ringing that bell. It might make

my wife uncomfortable. She's not bothered by smells, but they annoy her when they get pungent and impertinent."

Obediently, my father did his friend the favor and put the sprig down.

And that first afternoon was followed by others. Evaristo would leave the counter and go to talk in the doorway. My father, at the tail end of the afternoon, would begin to check his watch regularly: he knew that around six fifteen, Evaristo's wife would stand up, dry and long in the twilight of her corner, and cross from one end to the other the world of all their days. So by quarter after six my father would already be taking leave of his friend, promising to return the following day. Evaristo would agree, feeling spiteful toward his wife.

My father would turn in the street to watch the couple: Evaristo would still be standing in the doorway, looking into the shop. His wife, like a bird from the shadows, had seized the little money drawer and was counting the coins. My father heard, in the stillness of dusk, the coins knocking against each other as she stacked them on the countertop. Evaristo, leaving the doorway, would suddenly go stand next to his wife, an open pouch in his hand. The money poured in, ringing out again, but just barely, almost as if the coins were small pebbles. Then my father would watch the woman take the pouch from his friend and put it on like a bandoleer, the belt slung gracelessly over her breasts.

And she was the first to leave.

The weight of the pouch pulled her down to one side.

Meanwhile, Evaristo, who was also outside, began to slowly lower the metal screen. The screeching put the air on edge and the woman would despair:

"Just give it a yank, one yank," she would say. "It's not made of silk."

Then Evaristo would stop for a moment:

"My nerves aren't as fragile as yours," he responded, letting his voice fill with all his accumulated bitterness. "You know that by now."

Neither of the two realized that my father was watching, listening. They looked at each other defiantly. It seemed to my father that the afternoon sun didn't reach the couple. It fled from them as from a harsh knot of shadows.

"What you're missing are brains," the woman said to him, attempting to stand up straight to make the ballast of the pouch cease to exist in the world. My father watched then as she grew larger, like a long pole that had been held down by the wind and was just now regaining its freedom.

Evaristo turned to look her in the face: anger covered the dead skin of her cheeks, her eyelids, and her forehead with ash. She was breathing the dark air as if possessed. But Evaristo was not cowed: he held the lock to the screen in one of his hands.

"An animal," the woman continued, "would have understood me better. Not you. No, not you. You'll make me die of rage. That's what you're trying to do."

"The same thing every time," Evaristo complained with irritation.

"You're a withered soul."

Evaristo, hearing this, spun around to face the woman squarely:

"Those withered souls are sometimes birds, eagles no one suspects. I've told you that before, too. What I'm seeking is not your death, not to kill you, but a sky . . ."

"You talk like that because you haven't lived, because you're a simpleton."

"I dream of a valley. With the sky on the ground."

The night following that afternoon, my father could not fall asleep.

The moon was shining. My father went out to the street and strolled around the small, deserted plaza until he had tired himself out.

Another day, he got up thinking about his friend. He put off the business that had brought him to the town and went to visit him. It was morning. Evaristo was surprised to see him come in. But my father did not stop to greet him: he headed for the back of the shop where the woman sat. Later, he would tell us how he practically found a different woman from the one he'd seen in the afternoons. She was sitting on a chair and watching the street that was still untouched by the sun but already as bright as the day. When my father approached her, she stood up and quickly, with one sweep of her eyes, encompassed her world of herbs. Then, from the tables, a rich wave of perfumes reached my father, which made him reel. He held onto the edge of the table to steady himself. The woman watched him with curiosity. She spoke. She told him that in the summer, after being shut away all night, herbs, like females, are potent when they awake, like new. But as the hours pass, the combination of the air and the light wears them down. My father heard her voice like a thread of water trickling through mint. And now he went no farther. He returned to where Evaristo was waiting for him. They stood there for a long time without speaking. At last the sun entered the street and slid over the whitewashed walls. My father let out a sigh. On his face, as on Evaristo's, the reddish cast of the sun was subsiding. Noises of metal screens broke the silence, but then the street regained its tranquility.

"Don't let that woman fool you, Sanjurjo," Evaristo warned my father.

"I came here ready to talk to her."

"Don't be fooled. . . ." Evaristo said again.

A week later, Evaristo appeared at our house. My father received him with genuine pleasure. We children surrounded him to get a good look at him. I touched his suitcase, which he held in one hand, and asked him where he had come from. But Evaristo didn't hear me: my father was pulling him into the house while asking us to continue playing. I don't know how many more times Evaristo came to visit us, but they were few.

One day I stopped playing once and for all in the dirt of the street and became my father's assistant. Although by then we only saw Evaristo on occasion, my father spoke of him all the time, as if he had just spent time with him. Evaristo had remarried in our town, shortly after arriving and as summer was coming to an end. According to my father, everyone in our house, even the dogs that guarded it, went to the wedding. Perhaps all I remember, and not very clearly, is the music and the musicians, sweating as they played a waltz under the sun. But my father would relive the details, one detail in particular, with great emotion.

As Evaristo's best man, he was responsible for dancing

the first number, the first waltz, with the bride, a tiny girl compared to his previous herbalist. The music swayed the two dancers in the shade. In the sun, the brass instruments sparkled brightly and gawkers crowded the entrance to the small dance floor. As they spun around, my father watched Evaristo's happy face and the faces of the fools straining to see and he felt that this was the best day of his life, of all his years. But the music stopped. Then my father released the small girl and returned her to the groom who had walked forward to meet them.

"Not yet, Sanjurjo," Evaristo told them. "Not yet."

My father danced two more numbers.

Evaristo didn't return to the table where the bride's parents, my mother, and other guests were seated and where the wedding cake, crowned by two little figures, stood. Evaristo went over to stand in front of the gawkers, at the entrance. He looked sharp in his black suit, standing tall among the ragamuffins. My father saw him there and remembered how he looked when he was an herbalist: as thin as his wife, the flickering flame of his life unassertive and weak, as if smothered. But it had changed: now it was full and perfect, like a fire burning the widest path through the air.

The heat on the dance floor and the heat Evaristo was generating with his presence had been transmitted to the bride, who softened like wax in my father's arms. My father noticed the change: her initial rigidity, which had prevented him from holding her waist, was now altogether absent. And with confidence and joy, he began to draw her near. They were already playing the waltz a second time when my father felt something like an open window in his chest through which the perfumes and sun of that other body were entering, in abundance.

Evaristo was watching only him, as if the girl didn't exist or as if he intentionally wanted to leave her in the shade.

The final turns around the dance floor seemed eternal to my father. As if to dance them he had to consume, avail himself of, the life of all those present. In the silence that followed the music, my father heard, in the distance, the voice of his friend asking the gawkers to move back and let the air and the musicians come in. The musicians entered and found a place to rest on the chairs against the wall and my father, Evaristo, and the bride went to sit at the table, at the unoccupied places of honor.

Undiminished happiness reverberated in my father's heart as he attacked an enormous slice of cake with a spoon and veritable enthusiasm. The yellow dogs from our house walked onto the dance floor and circled a few times, sniffing at the dirt and the musicians' legs and instruments. My father's mouth was full, sweet. Later he would say that the unusual procession of dogs, one after the other, amused him enormously. It also made him very happy. And in his memory, he still saw them: they left the place buoyantly, returning to the sun, the heat, and the endless space outside, their backs on fire, shining like the edges of knives. And we ran to catch up with them, and my father watched all of us, dogs and children, as if on a movie screen.

My father, the bride and groom, and the guests finished their cake and were letting it settle, washing it down now and then with sips of soda. The musicians, their plates clean, too, were talking quietly in serious tones, their ges-

tures and movements anchored to the importance they
knew their art had for this and other weddings.

Evaristo interrupted them to call their leader to the
table.

"Acacio," he said, "I want nothing but waltzes. Very soft.
Because neither you nor your men are leaving here again.
Not until the sun is within arm's reach."

My father had never seen his friend dance. He had
imagined him to be clumsy, moldy from years of nights
dedicated to the herbalist's shop. But no, Evaristo turned
out to be a top-notch dancer and as such, one who never
tires. He got up from the table around three in the afternoon, taking the bride's hand and bowing courteously to
my father. Then, like all dancers in the world, he headed
for the center of the dance floor and struck the position for
dancing the waltz. The gawkers had returned to the
entrance like bees to the flower of music, which just then
was starting up again, soft and discreet. Evaristo knew they
were there—his back was to the door—by the hint of
darkness they threw over the white tablecloth, over the
huge island of leftover cake and the two little figures
perched on top. My father thought that Evaristo, sensitive
to the lack of air, would not hesitate to go clear the
entrance again. But Evaristo did not lift a single finger to
do so. And he began to dance. My father understood that
his friend was delegating the matter to him and, before the
waltz was over, he got up to resolve it. After clearing the
entrance, my father discovered us playing in the street with
the dogs. He called to us:

"Hey, kids!" he said. "Have you had any cake yet?"

"No," we answered.

"Good heavens!" he exclaimed, and quickly disappeared from sight.

The bride and groom danced for two hours. Until after five. My mother and father were the only ones left at the table. The others had left one by one after shaking my parents' hands by way of taking leave and apologizing. For it was a weekday and a workday. And because they were there principally because of my father, the only one in town who knew the groom. But my mother left, too, after the last of the guests and at the moment when Evaristo and the girl were walking back to the table.

My father remembered them as hardly seeming tired at all.

"Happy?" Evaristo asked my father. And then, to the musicians:

"Come over here, have a soda with us."

The musicians drank their sodas standing up, like sentries of the bride and groom. Then they went back to their instruments and sat in the chairs, legs akimbo. My father was still looking at Acacio:

"You played very well," he said, "as usual. As if for you, every time is a good time."

"No," the musician countered. "It was the waltzes, Sanjurjo."

My father sensed the smell of mint accompanying his words. And he thought of Acacio, of his melodious spirit flowing from his mouth.

"A waltz is nothing but a waltz," my father argued, wishing for more perfume to fill the air. But the musician would say no more.

The perfume was coming from under the table. With

his breaths of air the musician had propelled it like a sail-
boat toward my father. My father remembered how
sonorous the air was. He had spoken with Acacio as if in
private, as if they had been a yard or two apart. And so, too,
had Acacio. My father sought the source of the perfume
and looked at the bride and at Evaristo. Evaristo, sensing
he was being looked at, turned and asked my father again:

"So, Sanjurjo, are you happy because you danced the
way God intended you to?"

The sprig of mint rested between the girl's hands, in her
skirt, hidden by the tablecloth: my father watched as it
rose into the air and stopped, her hand holding it like a sun
in front of his face. His astonishment prevented him from
speaking, left him confused, eyes blinking.

"For you," the bride told him and lowered the sprig to
his chest. "For you, from us."

That was the detail. And when thinking back, my father
liked to place that detail above the wedding itself so that
it might illuminate it forever.

Evaristo's big day ended at sunset. The bride and groom
left the dance floor before my father and the musicians. My
father bid them farewell at the doorway. In the street there
was a trace of dust suspended just above the ground, and
the bride and groom sank their feet into it. My father
returned to the dance floor. He was holding the pungent
mint in his left hand. He stopped in front of the musicians:

"Acacio," he said. "Would you play me another waltz?"

"Whatever you like, Sanjurjo."

Evaristo widowed three years later. I accompanied my
father to the cemetery. The afternoon was full of sun, but
it was a lukewarm sun, like a dove swaying in the wind of

the sky. You could hear the wind in the dry leaves of the trees. I was now almost as big as my father. Standing behind him, I saw, over his shoulder, how grief was bearing down on him, harsh and silent, pressing him into the ground. Evaristo was standing in front of us like a desolate land, like the other end of the earth. The wind that came out of the trees blew against him, against his back, and stripped him, as if he were a tree, of the wrappings of the last two nights: the smell of chrysanthemums and candle wax and the burning wake. Halfway between Evaristo and us, the wind did a pirouette, swinging around like a bell, casting off those essences and spilling them into the open earth. From there, from the dark wound holding the body of a woman, my father and I gathered up what the wind had dropped and looked at Evaristo with renewed compassion. My father said:

"Evaristo is wearing the same suit he wore at the wedding. That's no good: it's like tying a knot around his pain."

Evaristo didn't want anyone to go with him when he left the cemetery. My father, however, insisted:

"True friends stick by you at critical moments like these."

Evaristo looked at me, then at my father, and then at his dead wife, who hadn't stayed put where we'd left her but had come along, following him, imitating the sound of the wind in the leaves of the trees.

"What you say is true, Sanjurjo," he acknowledged.

My father felt encouraged and placed his hand on Evaristo's shoulder.

"So, let's go," he said. "Walking will ease the pain."

"No, Sanjurjo. I appreciate it, but I have to go home by myself."

"Whatever you say, Evaristo. We'll be waiting for you at our house, when you're feeling better. Good-bye."

"Good-bye, Sanjurjo."

That's what my father said. But Evaristo never set foot in our house again. Nor did my father go looking for him at his house. We all understood that the friendship was over. The days passed. My father and I always hoped to bump into Evaristo and thus begin the friendship again. On occasion we spent more time than was necessary in the street, as if to favor an encounter and as if we were walking around calling out loud to the widower. But the days of autumn came to an end and winter limited our excursions. That was when someone told my father one afternoon that he had confidential information:

"Don't worry, Sanjurjo. Evaristo no longer has any friends whatsoever. He doesn't even leave the house, and when he does, there isn't a power on earth that can squeeze a greeting or a glance out of him."

My father stood there thinking. I read in his eyes his memories of the wedding and from still earlier times: when he met his friend.

"The thing is, that woman," he said, "that girl of his was the kind who knows how to sink deep roots. The Seed of God. The Miracle of God."

Later, alone, my father turned to me:

"We have to go look for him," he said.

Evaristo received my father cordially. He dispelled the shadows of the long months we hadn't seen each other when he said:

"Forgive me, Sanjurjo."

And then he began speaking to us of the dead woman. His voice no longer sounded the way I remembered it sounding in our house, on that afternoon in the cemetery. It had lost its middle range to the low tones of a stringed instrument. To play the instrument properly, Evaristo closed his eyes and moved his hands rhythmically in front of us.

Listening to him, night caught us unawares.

We took our leave of him, a blind man, sunken and quiet, like a stone in the darkness of the room.

On the way home, my father said that he didn't plan to visit again.

"The man makes me feel the girl's presence again. That's why. But you," he added, "you will go back to keep me informed about his health, how he looks. Because Evaristo is reaching the end and it won't be long before he dies, too."

But my father was wrong. He was the first to die. The day Evaristo heard it from my mouth, he didn't say a word about the woman. Sitting down, his chin covered by a scraggly beard fallen against the sadness of his chest, he began skirting around his memories. Some of them were similar to those my father had told me. Countless others were not. Evaristo seemed to be inventing them. The day passed us by. Evaristo got up from his chair and turned on a light.

But Evaristo, as if he hadn't heard what I'd said, returned once more to his memories. The light from the bulb bathed his face the way the noonday sun bathes a patio: the damage of being alone and the persistent memories were too much.

"Evaristo," I invited him. "Come with me tomorrow. I'm going to the cemetery. Your wife's grave is badly neglected. You could fix it up. Five years now. One of these days you won't find anything."

"Mercedes isn't in the cemetery, young Sanjurjo," he responded, and then, withdrawing his face from the light, he lowered it to his chest and closed his eyes.

"Come with me anyway. You could visit my father's grave, Evaristo."

"Your father isn't there either. . . ."

I didn't want to keep insisting and Evaristo picked up where he had left the thread of his memories. But not much time had passed when suddenly the lathe of his tongue fell still with a long sigh. That was when the perfume happened. It began to issue from all over Evaristo's body, from his slack mouth, as if from a fountain. It swept over me like a wave and I saw, through the green water, Evaristo's hands resting on his thighs. The shadows on his face reflected this very same color. Evaristo raised one hand and placed it on his chest, then tapped himself there lightly with his fingertips as if he were playing a drum above the water.

"They are here," he said, and he flattened his hand against his chest.

The perfumed water was now surrounding us on all sides. The light bulb was like a vegetable sun.

"They smell of mint," I murmured.

"Yes. They smell of mint," said Evaristo.

Translated by Mark Schafer

The Green Bottle

Ricardo Elizondo Elizondo

THE SETTLEMENT, hidden away in an isolated corner of the immense desert, had lost its population little by little. First to go were the men, those with sturdy legs and strong arms. Years before, they left in a flurry of revolutionary excitement, eager to fight for the right to own land. A happy affair all round, since nobody was fighting to own this stretch of land, the dry hilltops bereft of vegetation, the salt-bedeviled lowlands scorched by a sun fiercer than toothache. It was not long before the few men who

RICARDO ELIZONDO ELIZONDO (1950–) is an historian and novelist based in Monterrey, Mexico, where he is a professor and librarian at the Monterrey Institute of Technology. He has produced a lexicon of the dialect of Northeastern Mexico, *Lexicón del Noreste de México* (1996), and in 2001 UNESCO named him a Mexican member of the Committee for World Memory. In addition to his work in Monterrey, he has taught at universities in Texas, California, and Panama, and authored over twenty books on history and literature. His books of fiction include the short story collection *Relatos de mar, desierto y muerte* (1980), and the novels *Setenta veces siete* (1987) and *Narcedalia Piedrotas* (1993).

returned had left again, taking with them their possessions, their wives and children. This was a time of famine.
Once there were no strong backs to carry loads of lime and
alum crystals, the wagons that had once brought piles of
foodstuffs from the far side of the dry lake bed and gone
back crammed with rocks ceased to make the journey. The
times got so desperate that the old folks had to resort to
old Indian customs, so largely forgotten that they had to
virtually reinvent them. They relearned how to eat the
tough roots of bushes that barely reached knee-height.
They laid traps for snakes and burrowing vermin. One day
when the sickly children looked more wretched than ever,
the women got together and killed a wild mule that had
come wandering along the canyon. Since that time, the
more farsighted ones had taken to planting pumpkins and
beans, constructing shelters from the fibers of maguey
plants to protect the seedlings from the fiendish sun.

It was there she was born, though nobody could say
exactly where or when. All they recalled was that she was
the second daughter of the seven children her mother bore.
She grew up scratching away at the hillside and grinding
maize with a stone mortar. Hardened by carrying heavy
jugs of water, her shoulders were as tough as a man's, as
were her legs and slender feet. With her masculine strength
she could walk for hours on end, her head wrapped in a
cloth and her mouth covered. If there was need, she was
bold enough to go by herself to the farthest hilltop, until
she was lost from sight. And go she did. From childhood
on, she had grown used to death and to silence; she had
seen many lives shrivel to nothing, both children's and
adults'. Sometimes, in the burning noonday, blinded by the

sun, she wondered what lay beyond the glittering levels of the sands. She had asked the wagon drivers, but their reply was always the same, that beyond the sands were vast stretches of thornbush, and beyond them more sands.

The drivers had been only as far as the railway station, but they claimed, relying on hearsay, that after a thirst-defying journey of hours piled on hours, there existed a place where everything was green and the rain fell every day. She had serious doubts about the existence of such a place. One of the drivers had presented her with a bottle of green glass, the most wonderful present of her child-hood. She kept it wrapped in a clean cloth and every day held it before her eyes so that the dazzling dryness of the landscape took on the appearance of a total green.

She grew up quickly, always waiting for rain, always hacking away at the dry soil. At twelve, she knew how to raise an infant and what to do to avoid being a liability to her family. At fourteen, she recognized the presence of her man, and at fifteen, they settled down together. Her man was a fool, more stupid than a sun-struck hen, but she loved him and loved him well.

One windy morning, a little after the birth of her son, the drivers came with disturbing news. The men beyond the dry lands were talking of war, knives, battle cries, and horses. A grand struggle was in progress, men were gath-ering, there was free travel by train, the cause was a wor-thy one, and there was a guarantee of food and pay. Not to mention looting and other inviting perks, for there is truth in the old saying: "To the victor go the spoils."

These promises brought an eager light into the eyes of the lime-burners. "To buy you a pretty piece of cloth," they said to their wives, "that's why I want to go." Stubborn and hard as pebbles, the women stared at the ground, but then their eyes met their men's and they yielded. The following day, along with the wagons, the first batch of men set out, that evening a second batch, and on the third day the rest of the men. After two nights the community was stripped of husbands and brothers. They had promised to return soon, before the supply of corn ran out, but they failed to keep their word. Weeks went by and anxiety set in. Hunger stalked the hill country and before long the children were begging for food and playing less. Hunger was visible even in the restless glances of the old folks and in the tormented faces of the women. "Ghost of the drought, twisted root of mesquite," they chanted, "go away, go away, go far from here." But Hunger just laughed and every day danced its reckless dance of death. The only hope was that the wagons that came for the alum would bring food. While sinewy hands collected rocks, nervous eyes scanned the horizon in vain. The glittering piles of crystals and white stone grew higher and higher. One day they found an old woman crooning to herself where she lay cradled at the bottom of an empty container for beans. Then they left the salty rocks and set out for the acres of scrub and thorn. Their stomachs blazing with rage at their abandonment, they picked up machetes and chopped at anything that was edible. The older folks seized whatever came to hand. Rats, the knots of ropes, and dry vegetation kept them going for months, as, bit by painful bit, they once again turned into farmers.

It was nearly a year before the first of the men seduced by the revolution came back. He arrived exhausted, reduced to a skeleton, with nothing to show for his pains. He explained that things hadn't turned out as they'd been led to believe. They had boarded a train and traveled for several days until, one evening, quite unexpectedly, a band of armed horsemen stopped the machine. Everything was confusion. Those who were able to jumped down from the train and ran off between the magueys and the cactuses. They escaped the bullets but probably not the desert itself. "The rest of us," he went on, "kept quiet inside the wagons, which were as big as three huts put end to end. And it turned out to be the best move, because the horsemen asked us if we planned to put up any resistance, and which general we served, and who we were fighting for. The fact is we had no idea. All we want, we told them, are tortillas and beans and, if possible, something to spend on our wives and kids. They spread-eagled us on the rails and kept us there for a long time, until somebody more important arrived on a really big horse. From what we could see of him from the corners of our eyes, we figured he had to be the big boss. He kept staring at us. Then suddenly he tossed a rifle to one of us and the simpleton grasped it by the barrel. The big man burst out laughing and shouted that we were a bunch of fools and that we could relax our legs. It was nearly dark when they put us back on the train and by the time dawn was breaking, we arrived at a place where there were women and hot food. . . .

The whole night passed in the telling of his story. The woman and the old folks of the shabby settlement drank it all in with their eyes wide, anxious for still more news. By general agreement, nobody interrupted him; it was better to ask no questions, in case their informant lost his patience and with a single gesture of his hand extinguished the flickering light of their hopes. But then an old woman spat loudly and called out, "And my three horses? Where are they now?" Her question precipitated an avalanche of other questions over the man, as grief and tears overwhelmed the ears of his audience until they buzzed. She didn't ask him any questions but her man was mentioned in passing. "Just as I thought," she said to herself. "He was such a fool." Like the shadow of a vulture, she got up and with her skinny son asleep in her arms, sat at the door of her hut and chafed her ankles with her hands until she made the dry skin squeak.

The transport wagons never came back. Very few men returned. Those that did told her many things, but since she already knew the fate of her man, they all sounded like more of the same. She kept on working from before the sun was up. She deepened the well, while her son, a tiny thing, up above, yanked on the rope, which they had both woven, and hauled up the damp, sandy soil in a pail fashioned from a tortoise shell. Once, while looking for wild honey, she came across a rabbit with its litter. Instead of killing them, she chose to raise them. Miraculously, they thrived. After that, things got easier. She used the excrement of her dogs and rabbits to fertilize her small parcel of cultivable soil. She surrounded it with tough, spiny bushes to defend it against the onslaughts of the burning wind. There she planted maize, pumpkins, and beans, and fed a diet of grass and diced nopal cactus to the rabbits. In a few years, she was harvesting enough to make gifts or to barter. She then set her sights on a hen, but the only man who owned hens refused to trade her one and even shut them inside his hut to protect them. Finally, after many pleas from her, he agreed to trade one male and one female chick for four rabbits and a medium-sized bag of clean beans. The chicks cost her so much that for months she neglected her vegetable patch in order to watch over them. She used to send her son out into the tracts of thornbush to look for white worms and gray butterflies, and not until the chicks looked grown and vigorous, did she stop boiling the water they drank.

While she buried herself endlessly in work, the settlement was losing more and more of its population. At first she didn't care and paid little attention. Somebody's come, she observed, and tomorrow he's leaving with his wife and kids; the grandmother refuses to go, because, most likely, she'll die on the journey, but his husbandless sisters are going to go with him. Well, what do other people matter to my son and me? We have nobody in this world. As long as my son's strong, we won't go wanting for food. But then she detected that her son had a gleam in his eye and the same brave curiosity she herself had had as a girl, when she'd watched the transport wagons or smashed a snake's head with a large rock. She was afraid, very afraid, and had no religion to comfort her, because she had been taught none. Her son was as taciturn as his father had been, but he was not as stupid, by no means as stupid. How could he be, when just by thinking about it, he'd come up with the idea of using channels to water the land and thanks to him, they had their own bees to give them honey all year round? That was why she was so afraid he might leave in a fit of emotion. He was all she had. But she wouldn't hold him back if he wanted to go far away, though she would

shrivel away to nothing, working by herself, for there had
to be a wider world out there, beyond the last dry hilltop.

One night when she and her son were out in the yard,
playing hide-and-seek, they heard loud shrieks of women,
which could have been either laments or laughter. The first
thing they thought was that one of the elderly had died and
they unhurriedly sought the source of the noise. To their
great surprise, they saw, in the light of a tallow candle, two
pairs of trousers and two shirts of a beauty and color they
had never imagined. Around these novel garments, the
whole population was circling, a population now so scanty
it could have fitted into a single hut. She quickly recognized the visitors. One was her own brother, whom she had
given up for dead, having had no news of him for years. It
turned out that before the war had ended the pair had
headed far north, and there had found work with a lady
whose skin, they claimed, was very white and the color of
whose eyes matched that of her precious bottle. Their bodies were in fine fettle, their cheeks full, unlike those who
had made it back from the war. "You like my shirt so
much," said her brother, "that I'll give it to you for your boy.
And for you yourself here are some colored spectacles, so
that you can keep on see everything yellow as if it were
green." They had brought with them two bags bulging
with clothes and everybody got something. That night, of
course, nobody slept. They told her so many things that her
head started spinning. She thought it wisest to go outside,
and she killed a rabbit, seasoning it with traditional herbs.
Once it was boiled in water and salt, she served it on her
finest plate, chipped at the edges and darkened by use. She
offered it to the recent arrivals as the best thing that she

and the rest of the population of this salt-infested land had to offer.

The visitors stayed for two weeks. If she had known anything about the world at large, she would have found appropriate words to describe them, but she sought in vain, over and over again, among her restricted vocabulary for the adjectives right for them. They seemed to her like evangelists, preaching of a distant land of great promise and cursing bitterly the wretched patch of earth they'd been born in. Then what she had been fearing so much happened, and it hit her like a deafening blaze, even as it kindled the eyes of her son and changed him. Often, in those two weeks, she caught him watching her and she felt scorched by fear. Though she knew what he was thinking, what he was wanting, she distracted herself in order to avoid him. One afternoon, with everything in its place, with everything that needed doing already done, instead of remaining, as she usually did, in the shade of the hut, she told herself she needed to add another row of stones to the wall around the yard. "Better that than listen to what he's liable to say," she told herself. But the boy had already made up his mind. He waited for an hour, watching his mother's figure shimmering in the heat, floating between the blasts of burning light coming in from the sands, when the desert was at its worst, at its most threatening and unnerving. She knew it, she felt an immense stone poised at the mouth of her stomach; she refused to look back at the hut; she refused to think another thought. As stubborn and as mindless as a mule, she loaded stone after rough stone into the basket that hung from her shoulder.

The moment she arrived at the wall, with her back

always to the hut, she felt her son's arms encircle her tightly and heard his undisguised sobbing in the nape of her neck. Then she broke down herself and violently let loose the feeling she had been withholding: that she was a rotten bitch, plagued with worms, and selfish. Her guts collapsed and she released all the kindness within her. Out there, right under the sun whose stupefying heat reduced her land to a desolate exhaustion, she gave him her understanding and held nothing back.

Once more she saw men setting out toward the railway tracks. She gave him a little bag filled with the prettiest stones the desert had to offer but did not speak to him, for it was as if all her blood had clotted in her mouth.

Astonished and nervous, the boy climbed aboard the train. In addition to what he was wearing—all of it given to him by his uncle, who was accompanying him—he carried a cotton cloth folded to make a bag, containing dried and ground up boiled maize, biscuits made of beans and honey, thick chunks of mineral salt, small pieces of cactus leaf to use as medicine for any aches and pains, and the little bag of pretty stones. As the only movement he was used to was that of his own legs, the rocking motion of the train put him through a hell of nausea for two whole days. His companions advised him to keep his eyes on the far distance as much as he could, but his eyes, accustomed to looking down—the only way to avoid being burned by the sun and the wind—stubbornly reverted to the dizzying whirl of cactuses and rock formations that raced by, straining them and churning his stomach. Eventually, the rattling motion of the planks and iron frames became part of his flesh and his stomach adapted to taking in food while everything around him shook endlessly. Early one morning he heard the mighty machine squealing, first a little backward, then a little forward, then once again backward, and once again forward, and he felt so scared at the halting of the train that he woke his uncle. They had arrived.

There were so many houses, so many people, so many things crowding his mind that he couldn't find words for them. Astonishment piled on astonishment. He could not understand that there was still more to come. They walked across a long bridge built of stone, wood, and iron, and surely that was the end of it. For a while he had been encountering things he'd never seen before and had no name for, but at least he had understood something of what the people were saying. But now, not even that. People were talking as if they were imitating the clashing of knives or the clinking of plates. To the trembling of the train that he still carried inside him was added the trembling of fear. A snake twisted and turned in his guts and a swarm of flies buzzed up from his stomach into his head. Along with other men like themselves, they entered a huge corral fitted with benches, where sat still more men like themselves.

There they stayed until there arrived the contractors with what his uncle called the application. "Don't tell them any lies," he added. "If they ask you what you know how to do, show them by making gestures. They're going to strip you down, and then drench you with a stinking solution. You'll feel it burn your skin, but don't worry. Only the men who get disinfected are allowed through. They're going to check you, back and front, your head, armpits, and mouth, even your penis. Don't be scared. It's like buying horses. You have to check them thoroughly, to make sure you're not being suckered. Probably they'll take away your bundle, so give me anything you want me to take care of. I'm already on their list, so they're going to disinfect me, and that's all. Don't open your mouth or your eyes, because the stuff is poisonous. I'll see you at the exit."

They kept him for twenty-four hours in a white building. His skin was plagued by a burning sensation, as if he'd been rolled in the lime of his home settlement. "Just wet your face," they told him. "But don't scratch, or you'll open up burning sores." They gave him meat and potatoes and something unfamiliar: a glass of milk. He couldn't sleep. The itching was bad enough, but in the middle of the night, he suffered a stinking diarrhea, and his temperature soared and left him dizzy and faint. As stoic as his mother, he uttered no complaint. They woke up his uncle to tell him that the boy was in the toilet with his head between his legs. They took him to the hospital and gave him a white liquid that resembled the milk but tasted of powder. Even so he couldn't sleep. The next noon they once again gave him meat and potatoes and a drink of herbs that he really liked. That evening they lined them all up and handed out bars of soap. He had never seen such torrents of water before. "Wet yourself thoroughly," they told him, "and soap yourselves three times." He did as he was told, but even so, a week later, his skin still felt on fire.

The big truck that transported them to the ranch—at two days' distance from the border—was normally used to move pigs. The woodwork that made up the cage stank of old pig shit. He happened to be in the center of the standing human herd, which swayed from one side of the cage to the other, and through a gap in the bars he observed the marvel of constant greenness. His dark eyes learned many lessons, and all the while his hands longed to sink themselves into the juicy soil. He spent two months at the ranch harvesting potatoes, which they paid him for by the basket, then a month in the packing plant. He separated hundreds of potatoes into dark ones and light ones, and they paid him by the day. When that job was done, a truck took them to he-didn't-know-where. There he clambered up a ladder and on every branch of the trees he left between three and five peaches, depending, and cut off the rest. Once again the job was done, and again in a truck, but this time seated, they were carried off to cooler ground, where the air was scented by an infinity of walnut trees. The stronger men beat the trees with a long pole while he collected the nuts in baskets. In the evenings and even into the night he cleaned the nuts, and for that they paid him double: by the basket for collecting the nuts, by the box for cleaning them.

His uncle presented him with a belt pouch made from snakeskin and he never took it off, for he kept his money in it. He learned to count and knew that these ten pieces of paper with a certain fellow on it were worth that single one with another fellow on it, and that ten of those were the equivalent of one of the very special papers that had a bald-headed, bespectacled fellow on it. He preferred these last ones, because they weren't as bulky as the others and he could fit more of them into his belt.

He spent the whole winter on the walnut farm. Day after day he swept up leaves, put them in a grinder, and then spread the compost over the huge orchard, which was fenced in all around its upper reaches. A layer of leaves, a layer of soil, a layer of leaves, a layer of soil, endlessly, until it drove everybody wild with tedium except him, because he liked to work. In the middle of winter, something happened that he could not understand, but they told him that these bills were worth nothing or that those others were worth something.

Distinguishing himself from the general run of workers, he kept on rising at first light and, with his rake in his hands, worked over the grounds of the orchard. One day his uncle told him he was going to the city and invited him along. He took the invitation as an order. They walked as far as a broad highway and kept on walking along its edge. A fellow countryman they did not know gave them a ride in his two-wheeled cart and kept on talking at them until the time they left him. His uncle took him to a house full of women and men who were smoking and dancing. After a while his uncle said, "I'm going to take a piss. Wait here for me." His uncle kept taking a piss every half hour, until the boy felt like taking one, too. He followed his uncle and learned that pissing didn't mean expelling liquid but imbibing it. To the rear of the washroom was a door. There the uncle knocked twice. The door slid back and out came two glasses of yellow liquid. It was immature brandy. "Here, take it," said the uncle. "You need to learn about this. The guys at the top don't want ordinary folks drinking. So they've prohibited booze. But there's a way around everything. 'Specially when it comes to a drink."

He would have preferred not to drink, simply because the stuff stung his throat, but his uncle was his uncle. Four times they returned to the sliding door, but he could remember nothing after that, he heard himself telling the gentlemen who spoke like clashing knives. They were questioning him and very occasionally he understood something of what they said. He insisted that he had no memory of anything after the fourth drink. The men were the representatives of law and order, the janitor told him. They'd imprisoned everybody they'd caught, but a lot of people had gotten away. He inquired about his uncle, but nobody understood what he was saying. When they asked him what he was carrying in his belt, he showed them the blisters on his hands, and they read in his eyes his keen sense of honor. They told him that nothing bad was going to happen to him. They sent him to a school-cum-work-shop, where they corrected those who'd left the straight and narrow. Once again he threw himself into work, and within the year, he had mastered the craft of rough woodworking, as well as the skill of talking with his tongue wrinkled. He did not lose hope of finding his uncle. One day they told him that he now had a saleable skill and they set about looking for a job for him. He was hired by mail by a man who lived very far away and sent money for his trip. He left a message for his mother's brother, but nobody ever picked it up.

It was a sawmill, a very small one, compared to the huge forests that surrounded it. As soon as he arrived, without anyone telling him and instead of sitting around like the rest of the workmen, he began picking up the wood shavings and bark scattered in the clearing in front of the work-shop. Then he organized the barrels round the back. "My God, you're a good 'un," the old man told him, as he worked. "I can see we're gonna get along real well." He did not understand much, but from the man's tone and smile he knew he was welcome.

By the end of the month, he had replaced three of his own countrymen in the trust of his employer. In twelve months' time, he was the supervisor of those who spoke his language. The boss took him to the bank and explained, as best he could, that there they paid you for letting them look after your money. He understood and before the incredulous eyes of the manager emptied out his pouch, stuffed with the results of four years' work. "A tidy sum you got there, boy!" said the man. The name of his mother was registered as his beneficiary, she who lived in the settlement of lime, alum, and silence, at the far side of the wide river, in a wrinkle of the desert under the hammering sun, where the people spoke her language and she was waiting for him.

Three more autumns went by, and his bank account kept on growing. One sunny noonday, while the white men were whining about the heat, and the blond owner of the mill was lunching on corn on the cob, mashed potatoes, and fried meat, came a sudden cry, "Boss, boss, the logs have rolled!" Then alarms and shouts and the snapping of metal supports. There was nothing they could do. The supervisor who'd come from the far side of the wide river, the one who was all work and never less than quietly confident, was spouting blood from a rip in his stomach, as he lay trapped between the sweet-smelling might of the cedar logs.

The boss tripled the amount the dead boy had in the bank. His name and that of his mother were added to the long lists that hung in the offices of the border to the south. They remained there for many years. But the fact was that nobody ever read those lists.

In the early fifties the bank near the sawmill was absorbed by a powerful banking chain. The auditors discovered on their arrival that the account had tripled over the last thirty years. Interest paid on the original amount was now in its turn earning interest. The beneficiary had made no claim. So it went on, year after year. Whereas the sum had been a respectable amount in the beginning, it was now a hefty capital. They consulted the old owner of the mill, and he informed them of the searches for the beneficiary conducted in those first years, all of them fruitless. He authorized the use of the interest to finance a formal search for the sole owner of the money. The banking chain hired the services of an agency that specialized in locating property and persons. The investigator who visited the sawmill found few data, basically nothing of significance beyond those written in the document that named as beneficiary a certain woman in a lime-producing settlement on the far side of the wide river. There was no alternative but to travel, as early as possible, to the desert mentioned and from there, somehow or other, conduct a search.

A local man was hired by the foreign investigator to travel through the settlements of the desert. "You can take all the time you want," the foreigner told him. "You're looking for a woman who may be already dead. It doesn't matter to me whether she's alive or not. All I need is a clear statement of evidence. They pay me the same whether you find her living or dead. Right now I've had it up to here with all this flying dust. All I need now is to start shitting williwaws and rattlesnakes!"

It ought not to have been so, but it was. The barren lot where she had waited was turning into a stinking filthiness without relief. At the beginning it hadn't been that way. She hadn't known how or at what moment her son would come home, but in the peaceful mornings when the silence of the suffocating sun trap brought into the winding channels of her ear only the murmurs of her own life, she felt in the depths of her soul the breeze of a moonlit night and the strange warmth of one who waits with hope. It was later, perhaps after she buried hope, that the mornings started to acquire a bitter taste and the nights savored of abandonment. She was never short of work. Then she was cursed with a back she dislocated while breaking up waste ground for planting. As people left, she had acquired more land, but all of it of poor quality and scorched dry like her own. When her brother came, he told her to burn the weeds and all she could manage of the scrub and to toss the ashes onto the furrows, because ashes aided cultivation. Several times she did so, until she realized that the ash was good only for pumpkins, and after that she confined the use of ashes to the pumpkin patch. She also found more water and had the option of a better-tasting well. Apart from its superior taste, its clarity turned out to improve the boiling of beans. The cleaner the water, the sooner the beans went soft, she found. So she got more plates, more cooking bowls, and more cloths. From the huts that were abandoned, she went around selecting the best of what was left, lengths of iron, sections of metal sheeting, here and there a plank. Day after day, over the years, she labored, toting, dragging, and twisting stuff in hopeful enterprises. She added to her hut a broad canopy woven from maguey fiber and under it placed the rabbit hutches. On the south side, the coolest, she built a hen run and put a roof over it. From the two original chicks she now had ten laying hens and two roosters. Every three weeks she killed a chicken and except for the time her fowls were infested with parasites, she never went short of eggs to eat. On the departure of her son, she increased her workload and finished the day exhausted, drained by the sun and wind. The night was her refuge. She kept so busy by day that no sooner had darkness fallen than she was fast asleep, freed from thoughts about waiting, saved from tormenting her heart with suppositions.

All that remained were the elderly, the people with faces the color of sand and hair dusty with lime. Convinced that they would die there and that nothing or nobody would ever liberate them from the red-hot frying pan in which they lived, they formed a gloomy brotherhood and began to dig their own graves, an assembly of aged shadows wasted by the sun. Once the work of providing their daily sustenance was over, two or three of them used to go together and determinedly break through the hard layers of lime that formed the subsoil of the tiny cemetery in the mournful hillside. Between twisted roots and ashy shrubs, they opened up, handful by handful, what had once been the epitome of their hopes and was now to be their tombs. A damned earth, damned for never having yielded them an ounce of sweetness. A savage land, haunted by devils, which repaid every caress by spitting back thistles and lacerating thorns. Cursed, totally cursed, roundly cursed, like those noons of torturing fire that enveloped them, day after day. Not one of their number had ever known the gift of fresh fruit or the luxury of plunging into water and rolling in its transparent waves. It had never crossed their minds that such things existed.

For ten years the holes in the yellow earth were not used. They remained as they were, open to the heat. Then, one death followed another, and in one year three were buried. From then on, in the dingy half-light of their hovels, the fixed stare of saddened eyes awaited the long-expected visit of death. She alone resisted the resigned meaning of her neighbors' gestures. She dug her grave, because they all had done it, but while she heaved up the sharp rocks, she swore to herself, by all her years of solitude, that she would never use it. She had the strength to wait for her son. Even if it meant enduring horrors, it didn't matter to her, as long as he came back to see her. As a child, they had told her that elderly Indians used to prolong their lives by eating, while still warm, the pregnant wombs of female animals. "Well, I'll do even that, when the vultures start to gather," she told herself. "I'll eat the wombs of my rabbits, even though I feel the birth canal opening, even though I sense the young animals writhing in my mouth, and myself weeping inwardly. I have to live long enough to see him come back. There, over there where the train goes by, that's the way he'll come, loaded down with his own kids, and he'll take me away with him, because I don't want to die alone. . . ."

Her energy stayed with her for long afterward, even

when only two of them remained alive in the settlement, and the other, a man, was spying on her to see if she could still get out of bed in the morning. Solid in her conviction and hope, she was sure that she'd be the one to drag the neighbor she'd known all her life over to the hillside. And so it turned out. One evening she missed the trembling candle flame that indicated the presence of the man. She became aware that all afternoon she had been hearing a commotion among his hungry hens. Suddenly she was gasping for air; in her own inner ear she heard the rattle of chilling death, and her legs froze in terror. She found him stiff, with a thread of bloody spittle dangling from his mouth. A huge lizard was already sucking at his eyeballs.

She made a stretcher and in the morning dragged him to the hillside of oblivion. She came back, feeling as if she had turned to stone, her teeth reduced to sand, her hopes almost in ashes.

The passing of time became an obsession with her. She measured it by the molting of the hens and the flowering of the nopal cactus. Every night she seated herself in the yard, clutching a large bundle of rags in her arms and talking aloud to it. Sleep was harder and harder to come by, even when she worked hard. She spent the night watching the stars or imagining the children her son had fathered.

From the moment he came into sight in the far distance, she had been observing him, a tiny point in the monotony of the desert. She was drawing water, and long shadows were beginning to creep across the soil, while the breeze from the white-hot desert was also beginning its daily stroll. Her chest opened with emotion, and she felt the gap between her breasts threatening to burst with palpitations. All her muscles quivering with emotion, she raced to welcome him, without a cloth to protect her head, laughing like a lunatic and deaf with excitement. She ran weeping, burning him up with her eyes, treading between the jagged rocks and not feeling the thousands of scratching thorns. "My boy is coming!" Her hair and all her skin were alive as if with ants. Her throat had closed painfully. Her legs forced a way through the scrub and her thighs brushed aside the broad, glistening tips of the magueys.

Her eyes were used to scanning the distance. Long before the visitor, enfeebled by the sun, could make out anything distinct on the horizon of growing shadows, she already knew that she was not seeing the son of her memories, and a shocking taste of iron paralyzed her, leaving her like a hieroglyph sketched against the cobalt-blue distance where the night was beginning. She went back the way she had come, very slowly, and pulled coals from the fireplace and in the front of the yard lit a huge bonfire of dried maize stalks so the stranger might have a guide and his persistent thirst would be finally slaked.

"That's not my name and I don't know her," she assured him. "Nobody of that name lives round here. I've been living by myself for years now, just me and my rabbits and my hens. If there was anybody here with that name, I'd tell you, but there isn't, there's nobody. . . ."

Astonishment and pity filled the visitor's face. He had arrived sunburned, the corners of his mouth white with dust, his forehead reddened, and his hands cracking open like the earth under a drought. She knew full well the tortures of thirst and the agonies suffered by those who, after walking under that sun, swallowed water in reckless gulps, so she periodically gave him small sips of water with a grain or two of salt in order to extinguish, little by little, the fire raging inside him. She moistened some clean strips of old rags and placed them on his forearms, forehead, and the soles of his feet. She refused to let him speak or move. She kept on giving him water until the man said that the only way he could drink any more would be to vomit up what was already inside him. The blazing fire was a heap of ashes before she told him he was free to move and talk.

For the first time in many years, she prepared a hot supper. When she was alone, any uneaten food turned rancid in the pan, converted to vinegar and bubbles by the intense heat. The man talked to her about a migrant worker who had died at the age of twenty-four. He'd left a fortune to his mother, about twenty years before, and it was his job now to find the woman. "If she lived here once," she answered, "she doesn't now. She must be dead as dust, with her bones turned to saltpeter. There's nobody here, they all died long ago, there's nobody here."

After supper, the man fell asleep, and she stayed there, looking at him, feeling hollow inside. Then she set the rabbits free and scattered the hens among the ashy ruins of the abandoned settlement. She made up a parcel of cooked maize kernels, biscuits of beans with honey, a small flask of water, and a handful of the local salt. Before the early sun got hot, the man set out. She gave him the packet of foodstuffs, along with some old sunglasses, and, carefully wrapped in spotless linen, an old green bottle.

With the pain of years knotting every joint, she slid down into a sitting position. So many years of being there, breathing fire, sucking up water while crouched to the earth, caring for her sterile land. . . .

Next to the railway tracks lay an emerald bottle, shattered into a dozen fragments. Back on the cursed outcrop of alum and lime, hidden away in a wrinkle of the desert, a woman allowed herself to die as she faced the shimmering glare of the hot sands, faced the heat that had reduced her skin to paper and hardened her eyes to stone. She was dry, inside and out.

Translated by Geoff Hargreaves

Lady of the Seas

Agustín Cadena

HER NAME WAS CIELO, which means "sky," and she lived in one of those Baja California towns through which, by the end of the 1960s, it seemed the whole world was passing. At first it helped kill time, but she soon lost count of all the cars, motorcycles, and longhaired gringos who stopped to fill up on gas or buy something and then head on south. They were all going to the Sierra Madre, or even farther, to the Oaxacan coast. Seated on handmade Hopi-Kachina cushions, they would drink coffee or booze and

AGUSTÍN CADENA (1963–) was born in an Indian village in the Valley of Mezquital, Mexico. He is the author of twenty books of fiction, poetry, and essays. Some of his works have been adapted for radio and TV, translated into English, and published in literary magazines in the United States. He has received numerous awards, among them, the University of Veracruz National Prize, and the San Luis Potosí National Prize for Short Fiction. He has also received fellowships from Mexico's National Institute of Fine Arts and National Endowment for the Arts and Culture, among others. A critic, translator, and professor of Latin American literature at the National Autonomous University of Mexico in Mexico City, he currently teaches in Hungary.

talk about Ezra Pound and the communitarian nature of artistic creation. For them, poetry was a tribal bonfire and the poet should return to recite his cantos in the plaza. They would go on about this while watching the seagulls fly, and then they would leave. None stayed for more than a couple of days, even with Señora Gómez's cooking and the charms of the plump-cheeked and dark-eyed girls who waited on them in the restaurant. The heat, the flies, and the town's lethargy drove them away. Year after year, summer after summer, the sun parched the grass at the edge of the highway that overlooked the ocean. And year after year, Cielo had only Sundays to rest from the shrill ring of the cash register in the little grocery where she worked. On Sundays she went to mass in her neighborhood church where she sang in the choir, and afterward she would go to look at the ocean. She would walk barefoot for a while along the beach, feeling that this cold moistness on her feet was her portion of happiness for the week, and when the sun went down and the mosquitoes began to bite her arms and calves, she would put on her shoes and head home to get ready for the following week.

It was in the church choir that Cielo met Tacia. Although Tacia was a few years younger, Cielo liked her at once, for she loved animals, was obsessed with learning new things, and had a spontaneous and natural tendency to contemplation; but most of all, it was her way of laughing like a country girl, covering her mouth as if she were ashamed to show her teeth or to let anyone hear her.

As Cielo remembered it, the morning had been filled with sun. It was one of the first sunny mornings of the year, a day so festive that many of the hippies who were heading south took off almost all their clothes and went to throw themselves on the sand. From the hill where the church was, she could see the dark sand sprinkled with bright bodies braided together in endless kisses. At times, when the breeze from the sea changed direction and blew toward the hill, she could hear singing and the muted twang of a guitar.

"Wouldn't you like to go with them?" Tacia asked her in a voice so soft that no one else would hear. Cielo just crossed her arms. Tacia began to laugh in that funny way of hers, then moved away, toward the highway. Cielo followed.

"Are you going to town?"

"Yes. You, too?"

And they walked along the highway, without looking at the beach.

For several months, they went on meeting on Sundays at church. Soon they knew every small detail of each other's lives. Cielo lived with her sister in the oldest part of town, next to an enormous flour mill that hadn't operated in several decades. But her sister was rarely home; all day she worked in a packing plant and at night she came in to change her clothes and go back out. Tacia, however, still had both of her parents. She lived with them and two sisters and her grandfather, who was paralyzed. Until this time, Tacia's inner world had been nourished by his stories about Pancho Villa. The old veteran would relive his memories of the Revolution, when he fought by the general's side all along the border, and Tacia was much happier to listen to him than sit with her sisters watching the televi-

sion that never got good reception. Because of her grandfather, she got the idea she wanted to become a nurse—
even though her family did not have the money or didn't
want to pay for her studies. In any event, she took advantage of every opportunity to follow her vocation, about
which she was learning more all the time. Cielo, however,
had no ambitions for herself, but she admired her friend
and wanted to help her achieve her dreams. There was still
time. Tacia had only just graduated from junior high.

One morning Cielo felt dizzy and she had chills. By the
time she closed up the grocery, she had a fever. Her sister
had gone to party in San Diego, but Tacia was with her.
Defying her parents, Tacia went to take care of her sick
friend. She stayed up with Cielo all night, spoon-feeding
her medicines and watching over her sleep until her back
hurt from sitting up so long in the bed. Two days later,
Cielo was able to get up again, feeling that her sickness was
no more than a memory and actually a pleasant one, for it
was lit with the glow of affection, with smiles and words
whispered in her ear by a voice full of concern and hope.

It so happened that it was nearly midday when she
opened her eyes and saw the June light come in timidly
through the closed window of her sickroom. She felt that
she longed for air smelling of rain; she got up to open the
blinds. Then she got dressed and went out to the street.
They were not yet expecting her at the store, so she went
for a stroll toward the highway and then down the slope
that was covered with wet grass. Waiting stranded on the
beach was the only friend she had had until Tacia appeared:
an old iron boat, its hull riddled with holes and completely
rusted. Many times Cielo had come here to gaze upon it

and tell it her secrets. At the end of the afternoon, a few seagulls arrived to roost on the mast. Cielo heard them fighting and screeching for the best perch; she heard the slap of the tide that had begun to rise and she thought of Tacia, of her dark eyes filled with tenderness, and she felt that she would have liked at this moment to stop time.

She sat there on the sand for a long time, until the sun was a red line on the other side of the sea and suddenly, over the sound of the surf, she heard someone calling to her. It was Tacia, who had come looking for her, worried because she had not found her at home. Cielo said nothing; she stood and held out her arms, which were still weak.

Night surprised them there on the edge of the highway, innocently hugging each other, each protecting the other, and each noticing how the ocean, far in the distance, had begun to reflect the glittering darkness. The earth gave off a strong and sensual perfume.

Many times they hugged each other like this, their tenderness immense and cowardly, each inhaling the scent of the other, incapable of confessing what they felt. Maybe this was their way of protecting that feeling. Because love, while called friendship, can last indefinitely: it can survive an earthquake thanks to one of the most perverse kinds of hypocrisy. But when it recognizes itself for what it is, when love is called love, then, like Medusa, it turns to stone, a stone statue that soon breaks apart and crumbles. Yes. This is why they never spoke of it: they were afraid that their love would come to an end. And they were embarrassed and confused.

A few kilometers away, young people talked about free love and the girls went braless and would make love twenty or thirty times a day. But Cielo and Tacia were confused, and so they suffered.

Cielo was the older of the two and she felt responsible. She was the one who would have to put some distance between them. She started out by saying she was really busy, making up problems her sister supposedly had and that affected her as well. But she could not stop what had begun. One Sunday after mass, Tacia asked to come with her for a walk along the beach, and she brought her to where there was an abandoned ship. She demanded an explanation, and she began to cry. Cielo took her in her arms and hugged her with all her strength and the power of this secret and lonely love. She did not know what had happened.

September was mild in Baja California. The town awoke blanketed in fog, but it was not cold. And the afternoons were brilliant, golden. Someone on the beach lit up a reefer and began to recite poems.

When you are in love, you feel wounded by the slightest things; this is why it is easy to become ungrateful and cruel. Love is also made of this.

One day, without saying goodbye, Tacia left. These were the last years of the Vietnam war and the pressure of hippies and pacifists meant that there were ever fewer people for the front. Many Mexicans enlisted in the U.S. Army. Tacia offered her services as a nurse. But Cielo did not find this out until many years later, when the war was over and she saw her friend's name on a list of casualties. She had waited for her for so long. . . . She had waited for her on the beach, in church, in the grocery, every day, every afternoon. Even among the groups of hippies who came in to buy things, she would search for her face, her voice. Time went by and with it that whole world, that way of life. One day, a girl came into the store. She was wearing a multi-colored blouse and sandals and she had flowers in her hair and flowers painted on her cheeks. She bought some tomatoes and a pen because, she said, she was going to write a sonnet. When she left, a speeding car ran her down. She was already dead when the ambulance took her away. Cielo understood that this was the last of a race of young people to whom, who knows how, her friend had belonged. And she felt cold.

The following Sunday, while leaving church, an admirer offered her his arm and she accepted it. She was nearly thirty years old and she did not want to go on alone. They went to walk along the highway and then down toward the beach. The iron boat was still there, invincible, like a guardian. The man proposed that they climb up onto it, and this surprised her. It had never occurred to her to that it could be possible to clear this small stretch of water and storm this kingdom of crabs and gulls. Nevertheless, she did not want to; it seemed to her a kind of desecration. The more her companion insisted, the more stubbornly she refused. In the end, he contented himself by moving the boat a little bit and, with a penknife, scraping off the rust that covered its name. But for Cielo, even this seemed to her an attack on something that should not be touched. The name of the boat, like hundreds of others in North America, was *Lady of the Seas*. Cielo did not want to know it. When she turned her back on the beach and started walking toward the highway, the only thing in her mind

was to forget the past. In the last memory she allowed herself from that time, she saw herself lying naked on the
grass, covering her eyes with her arm and trying to catch
her breath, while Tacia looked at her and smiled, covering
her mouth like a country girl.

Translated by C. M. Mayo

Rancho Santa Inés: Fast!

C. M. Mayo

AT RANCHO SANTA INÉS there were no mules for our trip to Mission Santa María Cabujakaamung. The ranch hands had looked, but the mules had wandered through the desert too far in search of forage. Literally, they could not find them.

Nearing sundown, Alice and I sat at a picnic table under a thatched awning while the cook made scrambled eggs with *machaca* (shredded dried beef) for our supper. A pot of beans bubbled on the stove. The smell of the cooking wafted out from the open kitchen. The wall by the counter was plastered with bumper stickers: I'D RATHER BE IN BAJA

C. M. MAYO (1961–) was born in El Paso, Texas, raised in California, and came to live in Mexico City in 1986. She is the author of *Sky Over El Nido* (1995), which won the Flannery O'Connor Award for Short Fiction, and a memoir, *Miraculous Air: Journey of a Thousand Miles through Baja California, the Other Mexico* (2002), from which this excerpt is taken. In the heart of the peninsula's central desert, the far-flung Rancho Santa Inés contains the site of the last Jesuit mission, founded in 1767, the same year the king of Spain expelled that order from the whole of his realm.

read one; KILL A BIKER . . . GO TO JAIL. Several were from the Baja 1000 off-road race, which used the ranch as a pit stop. Alice and I were the only guests tonight.

A small, white poodlelike mutt nuzzled our legs. Palomito was his name, the cook said. A calico cat slunk up as well, meowing loudly. And her name? "*Gato,*" she said. Cat. She broke out laughing at me, that I would ask.

A capable-looking woman with short hair graying at the roots, her name was Matilda Valdez. She sat with us at the picnic table while we ate. She'd lived here for twenty-four years, she said. No, she'd never been out to the mission. Her husband didn't like her to leave the ranch house. "He says, you're a housewife, so this is where you belong."

As we spoke, the light faded. The ranch did not have electricity; Matilda lit a small gas lamp.

When we were finished eating, she sighed and rested her chin in her hands. "I would like to go to the United States," she said. "I like the style of life there. But I'm too old now. I wouldn't know how to live there. What would I do?"

In the morning, for breakfast, we ate eggs and *machaca* again; it was all they had. Matilda shooed away the cat, then went back into the kitchen, where she lingered like a shadow, washing dishes. At eight o'clock, it was already broiling hot. And strangely quiet—there were no chickens here, no goats. I watched Palomito sniff around our jeep, lifting his leg on each tire, and I thought of all the dogs that had marked them over the past several days.

"Doggy bush mail," I said.

Alice sipped her coffee. "More like message in a bottle."

Matilda's husband was named Oscar Valdez. Trim and

tough-looking, he had a pencil-thin mustache and eyes that peered out hard and slitlike from beneath a crisply molded white cowboy hat. On his belt he wore a turquoise-encrusted silver buckle.

I still had my hopes of getting to Mission Santa María Cabujakaamung. Was the road really impassable?

"*Es malo*," It's bad, Oscar said, "*muy malo*." It used to be better; he'd built it himself, together with his father and cousins in the sixties. But it hadn't been kept up; *chubascos* had washed out large sections. We could hike to the mission and camp overnight, he suggested.

We'd lost that time, I explained. Alice had to catch her flight from Loreto, to be back at work.

He swung a leg over the bench of the picnic table. Palomito leaped up and laid his chin on Oscar's lap. The mission was just ruins, he said, not much to see. But he had a picture in a book from the 1920s that showed the adobe walls still standing. Gently, he patted the little dog behind its ears.

A German film crew had recently come to make a movie about the mission. "They filmed what happened two hundred years ago when they sent the priests home. Then some others came and they took the Indians to Alta California. They put them all in chains. The actors wore soldiers' uniforms from then, very different from today!" He raised his eyebrows and smiled, and shook his head. "They had a book, and they were reading the history from that book, two hundred years ago! Oh, how can they know about this place and I live here!"

Oscar, I realized, was much more interesting than some old lumps of adobe.

"*¡Todo rápido!*" Everything goes fast now, Oscar said, fast! He wanted to tell me how things were before the Transpeninsular Highway was built. Before, he said, a car might pass by once a week, maybe once every ten days. "You could lie down and go to sleep in the middle of the road and nothing would happen to you!" He threw back his head and laughed.

Oscar may have looked slick—the big white cowboy hat, the flashy belt buckle—but he hadn't owned a pair of shoes, he said, until he was fourteen years old. One day, a mounted salesman arrived with his burro train from the sierras, selling shoes. Oscar had a bitch he liked, so they made a trade. "She was a good dog," he said as he stroked Palomito's curly white scruff. "But I really wanted those shoes. My first shoes."

When they needed to go to Ensenada they went on burro. "It took us two or three weeks. And sometimes I would go south to Santa Rosalía. I would eat at the ranches on the way for free."

There was no doctor. "You would ask yourself, am I sick? And you'd have to say, no, I'm not sick. Because if you are, well,"—he pointed to the yard—"there's the cemetery!"

He leaned over to the sugar bowl and raised a spoonful. "My father didn't know sugar until he was sixteen," he said, letting the sugar cascade back into the bowl. "'How can this be sweet?' my father said. 'It looks like salt!' He only knew honey."

"And bullets . . ." he said. "We only had a very few," *poquitas, poquitas.* "They were very expensive, my father would keep them wrapped very carefully in a handkerchief. We had to save our bullets for deer, because that was food.

If you were going to shoot a deer, you'd better aim well, kill it on the first try. You couldn't shoot coyotes or mountain lions, nothing like that." He laughed scornfully. "Not like today. Today bullets are cheap, they just go around shooting at whatever."

I mentioned the bullet hole I'd seen on the "golden spike" monument down the road at San Ignacito.

"I was on the road crew," he said proudly. He'd worked as a tractor driver for the local section. He'd been there at San Ignacito when the road crews met. "There was a big party. They gave us lots of barbecue, and trailers and trailers full of beer." The governor arrived with newspaper reporters to cover the ceremony. "There were a thousand people!" Oscar said, eyes wide. "I had never seen so many people in one place at the same time." That was in 1973.

The highway opened vistas for Oscar. Working on the road crew, he met people from other parts of Mexico. And instead of herding goats, he was able now to make a living from tourism. Every week Rancho Santa Inés had a handful of guests, not just Americans and Mexicans, but also Italians, Frenchmen, Germans, Canadians, even Japanese.

Now there were a lot of people passing through on the highway, Oscar said, all kinds of people. There had been a number of holdups, several bad accidents. Like most Baja Californians, Oscar was wary of mainland Mexicans. Some of them were good people, he allowed, but they had different customs. Many were drunks. Some of them would fight with guns and knives. "Here in Baja California," he said sternly, "we fight with our hands."

Bad roads, good people, goes the saying, good roads, bad people.

Now, strung along the highway, there was the hotel, the gas station, the trailer park. And added to all that, as of three years ago, they had TV, Televisa from Mexico City.

"Everything goes so fast!" Oscar said again. His eyes nearly disappeared in the creases of his grin. "*Fast!*"

Identity Hour

or,

What Photos Would You Take of the Endless City?
(From a Guide to Mexico City)

Carlos Monsiváis

VISUALLY, MEXICO CITY signifies above all else the superabundance of people. You could, of course, turn away from this most palpable of facts toward abstraction, and photograph desolate dawns, or foreground the aesthetic dimension of walls and squares, even rediscover the perfection of solitude. But in the capital, the multitude that accosts the multitude imposes itself like a permanent

---

CARLOS MONSIVÁIS (1938–) was born in Mexico City. One of Mexico's most prolific, witty, and insightful writers, he has published more than thirty books of fiction, journalism, biography, history, and social commentary. Among his many awards is the Xavier Villaurrutia Prize for *Los rituales de caos* (1995). His other works include *Entrada libre* (1988), *Escenas de pudor y livianidad* (1988), and *Nuevo catecismo para indios remisos* (1996). He is also the editor of a collection of Mexican short fiction, *Lo fugitivo permanece* (1985). The following essay is from the collection of his short works published in English as *Mexican Postcards* in 1997.

92

obsession. It is the unavoidable theme present in the tactics that everyone, whether they admit it or not, adopts to find and ensconce themselves in even the smallest places the city allows. Intimacy is by permission only, the "poetic licence" that allows you momentarily to forget those around you—never more than an inch away—who make of urban vitality a relentless grind.

Turmoil is the repose of the city-dwellers, a whirlwind set in motion by secret harmonies and lack of public resources. How can one describe Mexico City today? Mass overcrowding and the shame at feeling no shame; the unmeasurable space, where almost everything is possible, because everything works thanks only to what we call a "miracle"—which is no more than the meeting-place of work, technology, and chance. These are the most frequent images of the capital city:

~ multitudes on the Underground (where almost six million travellers a day are crammed, making space for the very idea of space);

~ multitudes making their entrance exam in the University Football Stadium;

~ the "Marías" (Mazahua peasant women) selling whatever they can in the streets, resisting police harassment while training their countless kids;

~ the underground economy that overflows on to the pavements, making popular marketplaces of the streets. At traffic lights young men and women overwhelm drivers attempting to sell Kleenex, kitchenware, toys, tricks. The vulnerability is so extreme that it becomes artistic, and a young boy makes fire—swallowing it and throwing it up—the axis of his gastronomy;

~ mansions built like safes, with guard dogs and private police;

~ masked wrestlers, the tutelary gods of the new Teotihuacan* of the ring;

~ the *Templo Mayor*:** Indian grandeur;

~ piñatas containing all the most important traditional figures: the Devil, the Nahual, Ninja Turtles, Batman, Penguin . . . ;

~ the Basilica of Guadalupe;

~ the swarm of cars. Suddenly it feels as if all the cars on earth were held up right here, the traffic jam having now become second nature to the species hoping to arrive late at the Last Judgment. Between four and six o'clock in the morning there is some respite, the species seems drowsy . . . but suddenly everything moves on again, the advance cannot be stopped. And in the traffic jam, the automobile becomes a prison on wheels, the cubicle where you can study Radio in the University of Tranquillity;

~ the flat rooftops, which are the continuation of agrarian life by other means, the natural extension of the farm, the redoubt of Agrarian Reform. Evocations and needs are concentrated on the rooftops. There are goats and hens, and people shout at the helicopters

*Editor's Note: Teotihuacan was the Aztec capital, now the site of downtown Mexico City.
**Editor's Note: The Templo Mayor, or Great Temple, contains the ruins of the Aztec temples to Huitzilopochtli, god of war and Tláloc, god of rain.

because they frighten the cows and the farmers milking them. Clothes hang there like harvested maize. There are rooms containing families who reproduce and never quite seem to fit. Sons and grandsons come and go, while godparents stay for months, and the room grows, so to speak, eventually to contain the whole village from which its first migrant came;

~ the contrasts between rich and poor, the constant antagonism between the shadow of opulence and the formalities of misery;

~ the street gangs, less violent than elsewhere, seduced by their own appearance, but somewhat uncomfortable because no one really notices them in the crowd. The street gangs use an international alphabet picked up in the streets of Los Angeles, fence off their territories with graffiti, and show off the aerial prowess of punk hairstyles secure in the knowledge that they are also ancestral, because they really copied them off Emperor Cuauhtemoc. They listen to heavy metal, use drugs, thinner, and cement, destroy themselves, let themselves be photographed in poses they wish were menacing, accept parts as extras in apocalyptic films, feel regret for their street-gang life, and spend the rest of their lives evoking it with secret and public pleasure.

The images are few. One could add the Museum of Anthropology, the Zócalo at any time (day or night), the Cathedral and, perhaps (risking the photographer), a scene of violence in which police beat up street vendors, or arrest youngsters, pick them up by the hair, or swear that they have not beaten anyone. The typical repertoire is now complete, and if I do not include the mariachis of Plaza Garibaldi, it is because this text does not come with musical accompaniment. Mexico City: another great Latin American city, with its seemingly uncontrollable growth, its irresponsible love of modernity made visible in skyscrapers, malls, fashion shows, spectacles, exclusive restaurants, motorways, cellular phones. Chaos displays its aesthetic offerings, and next to the pyramids of Teotihuacan, the baroque altars, and the more wealthy and elegant districts, the popular city offers its rituals.

ON THE CAUSES FOR PRIDE
THAT (SHOULD) MAKE ONE SHIVER

It was written I should be loyal to the nightmare of my choice.

JOSEPH CONRAD, *Heart of Darkness*

Where has that chauvinism of old gone for which, as the saying goes, "There is nowhere like Mexico?" Not far, of course: it has returned as a chauvinism expressed in the language of catastrophe and demography. I will now enumerate the points of pride (psychological compensation):

~ Mexico City is the most populated city in the world (the Super-Calcutta!);

~ Mexico City is the most polluted city on the planet, whose population, however, does not seem to want to move (the laboratory of the extinction of the species);

~ Mexico City is the place where it would be impossible for anything to fail due to a lack of audience. There is public aplenty. In the capital, to counterbalance the lack of clear skies, there are more than enough inhabitants, spectators, car-owners, pedestrians;

 Mexico City is the place where the unlivable has its rewards, the first of which has been to endow survival with a new status.

What makes for an apocalyptic turn of mind? As far as I can see, the opposite of what may be found in Mexico City. Few people actually leave this place whose vital statistics (which tend, for the most part, to be short of the mark) everyone invents at their pleasure. This is because, since it is a secular city, after all, very few take seriously the predicted end of the world—at least, of *this* world. So what are the retentive powers of a megalopolis that, without a doubt, has reached its historic limit? And how do we reconcile this sense of having reached a limit with the medium- and long-term plans of every city-dweller? Is it only centralist anxiety that determines the intensity of the city's hold? For many, Mexico City's major charm is precisely its (true and false) "apocalyptic" condition. Here is the first megalopolis to fall victim to its own excess. And how fascinating are all the biblical prophecies, the dismal statistics, and the personal experiences chosen for catastrophic effect! The main topic of conversation at gatherings is whether we are actually living the disaster to come or among its ruins; and when collective humor describes cityscapes, it does so with all the enthusiasm of a witness sitting in the front row at the Last Judgement: "How awful, three hours in the car just to go two kilometers!" "Did you hear about those people who collapsed in the street because of the pollution?" "In some places there is no more water left." "Three million homes must be built, just for a start. . . ."

The same grandiose explanation is always offered: despite the disasters, twenty million people *cannot leave Mexico City or the Valley of Mexico, because there is nowhere else they want to go; there is nowhere else, really, that they can go.* Such resignation engenders the "aesthetic of multitudes." Centralism lies at the origins of this phenomenon, as does the supreme concentration of powers—which, nevertheless, has certain advantages, the first of which is the identification of liberty and tolerance: "I don't feel like making moral judgments because then I'd have to deal with my neighbors." Tradition is destroyed by the squeeze, the replacement of the extended family by the nuclear family, the wish for extreme individualization that accompanies anomie, the degree of cultural development, the lack of democratic values that would oblige people to— at least minimally—democratize their lives. "What should be abolished" gradually becomes "what I don't like."

To stay in Mexico City is to confront the risks of pollution, ozone, thermic inversion, lead poisoning, violence, the rat race, and the lack of individual meaning. To leave it is to lose the formative and informative advantages of extreme concentration, the experiences of modernity (or postmodernity) that growth and the ungovernability of certain zones due to massification bring. The majority of people, although they may deny it with their complaints and promises to flee, are happy to stay, and stand by the only reasons offered them by hope: "It will get better somehow." "The worst never comes." "We'll have time to leave before the disaster strikes." Indeed, the excuses eventually become one: outside the city it's all the same, or worse. Can there now really be any escape from urban violence, over-population, industrial waste, the greenhouse effect?

Writers are among the most skeptical. There are no anti-utopias; the city does not represent a great oppressive weight (this is still located in the provinces) but, rather, possible liberty, and in practice, nothing could be further from the spirit of the capital city than the prophecies contained in Carlos Fuentes's novel *Christopher Unborn* and his short story "Andrés Aparicio" in *Burnt Water*. According to Fuentes, the city has reached its limits. One of his characters reflects:

> He was ashamed that a nation of churches and
> pyramids built for all eternity ended up becoming
> one with the cardboard, shitty city. They boxed
> him in, suffocated him, took his sun and air away,
> his senses of vision and smell.

Even the world of *Christopher Unborn* (one of ecological, political, social, and linguistic desolation) is invaded by fun (*relajo*). In the end, although the catastrophe may be very real, catastrophism is the celebration of the incredulous in which irresponsibility mixes with resignation and hope, and where—not such a secret doctrine in Mexico City—the sensations associated with the end of the world spread: the overcrowding is hell, and the apotheosis is crowds that consume all the air and water, and are so numerous that they seem to float on the earth. Confidence becomes one with resignation, cynicism, and patience: the apocalyptic city is populated with radical optimists.

In practice, optimism wins out. In the last instance, the

advantages seem greater than the horrors. And the result is: *Mexico, the post-apocalyptic city*. The worst has already happened (and the worst is the monstrous population whose growth nothing can stop); nevertheless, the city functions in a way the majority cannot explain, while everyone takes from the resulting chaos the visual and vital rewards they need and which, in a way, compensate for whatever makes life unlivable. Love and hate come together in the vitality of a city that produces spectacles as it goes along: the commerce that invades the pavements, the infinity of architectonic styles, the "street theatre" of the ten million people a day who move about the city, through the Underground system, on buses, motorbikes, bicycles, in lorries and cars. However, the all-star performance is given by the loss of fear at being ridiculed in a society that, not too long ago, was so subjugated by what "others might think." Never-ending mixture also has its aesthetic dimension, and next to the pyramids of Teotihuacan, the baroque altars, and the more wealthy and elegant districts, the popular city projects the most favored— and the most brutally massified—version of the century that is to come.

Translated by John Kraniauskas

One-Way Street

Juan Villoro

FOR YEARS, MEXICO CITY's zip code 20 was a vast bed of lava inhabited by squirrels, field rats and badgers. In the '70s, the whole area was conquered by a species with bank accounts in the eight figures. Alfonso was born in this neighborhood where the streets were named as they might have been in Paradise: Fuego (Fire), Cascada (Waterfall), Roca (Rock). In the full bloom of youth he had attained what might have appeared to be an attribute of his elders: the boredom of an oyster. His life was a tranquil siesta after a meal. He kept himself entertained by smoking the slim, mahogany-colored cigars he'd first seen Kojak smoking on TV, and downing the world's best flavorless drink: Perrier water.

JUAN VILLORO (1956–) was born and lives in Mexico City. Among his many books are the short story collection *La casa pierde* (1999), which won the Xavier Villaurrutia Prize, and the novels *El disparo de Aragón* (1995) and *El testigo* (2005). He has also written a best-selling book for children, *El profesor Zíper y la fabulosa guitarra,* and a travel memoir, *Palmeras de la brisa rápida: un viaje a Yucatán* (1989). This story is from his collection *Tiempo Transcurrido* (1986).

But he knew that, sooner or later, something unexpected was going to happen, and it would launch him into Real Life: tough, risky, relentless.

The first thing that interested him about punk was that it took work to get the details right; only those who were in on what was happening in London and New York knew about the latest movement in rock and roll.

For Alfonso music was like trying to juggle. He would put the records on his quadraphonic stereo that had to be listened to with rapt attention. He was surprised that Rick Wakeman could play so many keyboards at the same time, and that Carl Palmer could sustain a drum solo for twenty minutes. Only real virtuosos could play progressive rock.

With the punk revolt, rock had become a free-for-all. Any hot-blooded guy could pick up a guitar and do it. For punks, "professionalism" was the word in the dictionary that most made them want to puke. To hell with a beat and scored notebooks: rock is to use; rock is to wear out.

"We hate everything!" shouted Johnny Rotten, leader of the Sex Pistols, and from this moment, Alfonso knew that Alka Seltzer could no longer soothe his stomach and Valium couldn't calm his nerves: progress and civilization had lost their painkilling effect.

To be a punk, the first thing he needed was an alias. Criticism of contemporary society began with the destruction of the cult of the personality. The thing to do was make your name a sneer. Alfonso considered the possibility of using Poncho Ojete (Poncho Asshole), but no; he was punk, not low class. Finally he decided on Phonsy Asshole. His metamorphosis had been achieved.

Nonetheless, it was not easy to live as Phonsy Asshole. When he went out walking down the main street of the Pedregal, his mind was filled with ideas for punk acts: he could go to a pub and fling a pint of beer at some man in a Derby hat and a handle-bar mustache, sidle up to a pretty girl with green hair in Portobello, fight with drunken hooligans in Chelsea, spend the day in the Virgin Records store listening to the LPs for free. Alas, the landscape was quite different. Phonsy watched uniformed servants walking hunting dogs, construction workers sitting on the curb putting together their lunch, girls licking aseptic ice creams. Phonsy Asshole was a punk who wanted to fight; fists clenched; he was ready to twist the tits of some lord and say "gimme five kindsa cigarettes." Nevertheless, the only thing the world offered him was a horizon full of dogs making copious pees on shrubs.

But he did not lose heart. Thanks to records of the Sex Pistols, the Damned, and the Clash, he learned to sing as if he had a throat full of cornmeal. He managed to arrange his face into a slack expression, as if he were suffering from salmonellosis, and he sent away to England for soldering goggles, jackets covered with diagonal zippers, hair dyes, and safety pins that appeared to pierce his cheek.

Once outfitted, he flew to New York and London to visit CBGB, the 100 Club, the Marquee, and the other clubs where punk was coming hot out of the oven. He saw Blondie in underwear the color of bougainvilleas. He saw

Iggy Pop stab himself with a switchblade. He saw Sid Vicious dancing pogo. He saw the members of Devo moving like androids on strings.

When he came back to Mexico, he had the necessary know-how to put together his own band. He went over some punks' biographies. David Vanian worked as a gravedigger; Johnny Fingers was expelled from school for showing up in pajamas; Mick Jones lived in an orphanage after his parents abandoned him when he was four years old. Phonsy's friends had the vacant expressions of babies who had ingested an overdose of cereal. Nonetheless, in Mexico punk could not be something for poor people—for them, there were the funky dives. Punks were rebelling against the feeling that life was already over, against the apathy that comes from having everything: There is no future! Only friends of Phonsy could criticize capitalism's boring achievements. It was easy to convince them to participate in this rich experience. And so they got together as One-Way Street. In the mornings, Alfonso, Geras, Cheto, and Pipo studied at the Ibero University. In the afternoons, Phonsy Asshole, Billy Bloody, Chet Off, and Kevin Pimp sweated out adrenaline in One-Way Street.

Before making their debut as musicians, they went to the Plaza Universidad shopping mall dressed as punks. They drank coffee with cinnamon buns in Sanborns. They tried on shoes at Florsheims. They asked the price of a harpoon in Martí's Sporting Goods. People stared at them; no one could keep their eyes away from those four ridiculous-looking boys. Alas, no one said, "There are the punks, the rebels from the unemployment offices, the ones who stand against the paternalistic State and the dole." No, they whispered: "Look at those guys. Are they homosexuals? Maybe they're actors and there's a candid camera."

It was the same when they started to play. The audience seemed to be incapable of getting into this sound that had all the musicality of an electric pencil sharpener. Desperate, Phonsy smashed a beer bottle on the amplifiers and rubbed the broken glass over his chest until a slash of blood was added to the design on his T-shirt.

One-Way Street began to have success.

At the next concert, the audience greeted them with the kind of shouts heard at wrestling matches: "Smash it! Smash it! Smash it!"

Once again Phonsy had to use the broken bottle.

By the end of the month he had as many cuts as a bull fighter. But he didn't give a shit. What's more, there were a number of chicks ready to smooth mother-of-pearl lotion on his scars.

Nevertheless, the feeling of rebellion continued to be ignored. The topics of the day were different. People talked about the presidential succession, the breakup of the Polivoces TV comedy duo, and how ugly those new hundred peso bills were.

When the Christmas pageants began, Phonsy had already stopped dreaming of his anarchist's utopia. People were chewing *tejocotes*, passing out sugar-covered nuts and dried fruits, sucking sugar cane from the sides of their mouths. The Christmas spirit kept Phonsy, who was participating in the pageant, from slashing himself, and what's more, he agreed to sing "Away in a Manger," after having performed "Fuck Off." The other members of One-Way Street were also holding candles that dripped wax on their hands. Phonsy and his friends knew that never again would they go back to being punks.

When he left the party, as a farewell, Phonsy wanted to commit one last punk act. He called some policemen motherfuckers. In this instant he broke with the rules of bourgeois democracy, with the hypocrisy of liberalism, with that shithead John Locke. The policemen answered with a series of blows from their billy clubs. He shouted that—"AAAAA!"—he was a citizen with—"UUUUH!"—individual rights, but in vain. When people came out of the party they found him made into the perfect model for a "True Crime" episode. A patrol car pulled up next to him and they were about to take him to jail—but, fortunately, Cheto happened to have a Ministry of the Interior ID that his father had given him, and it was only this laminated rectangle that kept Phonsy, who was now once again Alfonso, from being arrested. Every inch of his bruised body had reverted to its true identity. With his cheek pressed into the street, Alfonso had a clear vision of the future.

Adios to the dangerous life. The next day he was sitting in a canvas chair with a BB gun in his hands, watching over the garden of his house, keeping an eye out for the squirrels, badgers, and field rats that threatened to take back their lost paradise.

Translated by C. M. Mayo

Oh, Polanco!

Guadalupe Loaeza

WHO TOOK AWAY its peacefulness, its prestige as a residential neighborhood? Who wiped off its face and repainted it with signs in all colors and flavors? Now: a business district full of boutiques, government offices, taco stands, supermarkets, unisex beauty salons, movie clubs, hotels, crêpe restaurants, and tire repair shops. Before, not so long ago: a neighborhood of philosophers, poets, writers. Beneath a freshly laundered sky, streets with names like Horacio and Homero led us, as if by the hand, to the Parque de los Venados (Park of the Deer).

As Li Liu Ling would say, do not ask me how time passes. There was a time when, as a little girl in the Cuauhtemoc neighborhood, I dreamed of Polanco. From there it seemed one could see the volcanoes; the sun and moon shined more brightly; the taste of an ice cream lasted

GUADALUPE LOAEZA (1946–) was born and lives in Mexico City. Journalist, radio talk-show host, screenwriter, and novelist, Loaeza has published eighteen books, among which her best known are *Las niñas bien* (1985), *Las reinas de Polanco* (1986), *Compro, luego existo* (1992), and most recently the novel *Las yeguas finas* (2003).

twice as long; one could buy more things for the same money. The people who had the privilege of living there were happier, more orderly, better educated, better dressed. It seemed to me that in Polanco everyone was happy. Its poor won the lottery and its rich filled their houses with lilies painted in pastels of all colors.

When I was thirteen, there was nothing I liked better than to visit my recently married sister. To step down from the Juárez-Loreto bus at the corner of Horacio and Tennyson was like entering the garden where the queen in *Alice in Wonderland* was playing croquet. I would walk the three blocks, my heart soothed and light. Far behind lay the polluted rivers of the Cuauhtemoc neighborhood. Polanco was elegant, sophisticated, exclusive, different, but above all, residential. The houses all looked like Wilber von Snobble's—the rich boy in "Little Lulu." I imagined that inside there were salons, butlers, candles, and TV rooms that went on into infinity.

The most important experiences of my adolescence took place in Polanco. There, in the theater of the same name, I saw my first movie not meant for children. *Teenagers* was its title. Nervously eating popcorn, I watched as Troy Donahue led the girl to a cabaña hidden in the forest. It was rated "B" according to the pages handed out by the Church of La Votiva. We climbed into a Mercury, and in the dim light of the Club Mundet parking garage, Pepe, my boyfriend, gave me my first kiss on the lips.

The first time I took off my socks so that it would appear I had on panty hose was to go to a charity fair at the Instituto Patria. Ofelia was my first wealthy friend who was lucky enough to live in Polanco, in a house that seemed to have two hundred all-white windows. The first dirty joke I heard was in the ladies' room of the Ariel movie theater. I still remember it and blush. Miss Sofía, my third-grade teacher, lived on Sófocles and, ever since I met her, I knew she lived in Polanco. I went ice-skating in Mexico for the first time where the Liverpool department store now stands. That is why I always feel cold when I go shopping. My greatest delight was to go into La China and leaf through the latest issues of *Vogue* and *Seventeen*. To me, the hamburgers at Klein's tasted of heaven; I was crazy for their french fries. My favorite dessert was at the Coronado: donuts with powdered sugar.

One day an invitation arrived at my house. It was from the Cuevas family who lived in what is now the Hacienda de los Morales. The party was formal and in Polanco. Thanks to the Polanco market, which is in the same place it has been for years, I ate cherries in Mexico for the first time. One week, I was putting together the money to buy my first Pat Boone record. With my wallet stuffed with bills, I took the Juárez-Loreto and bought my present in the Polanco record store. The first time I was followed in the street by someone with bad intentions was at the corner of Fundición (now Rubén Darío) and Tres Picos. I recall one very sad Saturday, much sadder than the others because Pepe was not speaking to me. It happened in Polanco, in the Colima Juice Bar, while I was languidly sipping a mango juice that was too cold for the temperature in my heart. "Let's go bowling," said my long-time friend Gabriela. And we went to Polanco's bowling alley, the one in front of Sears. I had never felt more of a "Polanquera," and had never been so happy. One day I decided to color

my hair the same as Brigitte Bardot's. I thought: "Only in
a Polanco beauty salon will they know how to get the color
just right." It was recommended that I get an appointment
chez Noël. Ever since, I have continued to color my hair *à
la* B.B. in Polanco. My first important sin, which I com-
mitted when I was fifteen, I confessed to a priest in San
Agustín. I was certain that the priests of Polanco had much
better judgment than those of Cuauhtemoc, and especially
better than those of the Río Po church. I will never forget
the first time I went to the house of an ex-politician, on
Presidente Mazarik Avenue. I remember, it impressed me
deeply. "Only in Polanco can one conceive of such a house,"
I told myself as I toured the jai alai court, the steam bath,
the library, the dressing rooms and game rooms, the dozens
of bedrooms, laundry rooms, and gardens. They even had
a real barber's chair. The frames of the doors and the windows appeared to have been crafted by an extraordinary
pastry chef from Sanborns. "This is California Style," my
friend very proudly explained to me. She was the granddaughter of the owners, and she also lived in Polanco.
There were seven cars in the garage. All appeared to have
been recently waxed and they were very long. There were
an Oldsmobile, a Pontiac, a Packard, a Studebaker, a
Thunderbird, a Cadillac, and an Opel. "Does each of these
cars have its own chauffeur?" I asked, intrigued. "I don't
know, probably," she said, arranging her crinoline, which
was full of tiny bells.

That house is now an enormous bank, which, no doubt,
would accommodate all the world's account holders. In
what had been the garage there are now Corsars, LTDs,
Volkswagens, and one or another patrol car. I have not

gone back to visit my crinolined friend. The last time I ran into her, she told me she was going to live in La Jolla because these days, living in Mexico City and, above all, Polanco, was crazy.

This is why now, when I go down Presidente Mazarik Avenue near what had been the house of my friend's grandparents, I hear in the distance the tiny bells of her crinoline.

Translated by C. M. Mayo

The Emperor in Miravalle

Fernando del Paso

FROM THE TERRACE of Chapultepec Castle, one can see the whole Valley of Mexico; above all, on a late afternoon such as that one — so clear, the air so transparent. El Paseo de la Emperatriz, shooting in from the east, almost to the foot of the hill beneath the castle. To the north, the Calzada de la Verónica. Toward the southeast could be seen the snow-capped volcanoes. To the south, Mount Ajusco. On a day such as that one, so transparent, one could even see some of the outlying towns. To the north, San Cristóbal Ecatepec; to the east, Los Remedios, Tacubaya. To the

FERNANDO DEL PASO (1935–) was born in Mexico City and studied economics at the National Autonomous University of Mexico. His novels include *José Trigo* (1966), which won the Xavier Villaurrutia Prize; *Palinuro de México* (1976), which won the Mexican Novel Prize and the Prize for the Best Foreign Novel Published in France (1985); *Noticias del Imperio* (1986), and *Linda 67* (1995). Also an essayist, poet, journalist, painter, and diplomat, del Paso was awarded Mexico's National Award for Arts and Letters in 1991. The following excerpt is from a chapter of *Noticias del imperio*, his widely lauded epic novel of Maximilian von Habsburg's doomed Mexican empire.

south, Mixcoac and its colorful fruit trees, and San Angel
and Tlalpan. And the rivers, which seemed to climb the
mountains and the forests full of the Weymouth pines
Countess von Kollonitz had so liked, and whose trunks, she
said in her memoirs, were entangled with begonias.
According to her, Mexican cedars were more beautiful and
ornamental than Lebanon's own. They were different than
the trees in Chapultepec Forest: from the foot of the castle
they spilled their dark verdure to the west. The valley's lakes
sparkled: Chalco and Xochimilco, Xaltocan, Texcoco. . . .

"... and thus how is it not possible, Commodore, to tell
one giraffe from another, or one donkey from another donkey, I swear it, *parole d'honneur*, I could not tell one Negro
from the next. They are all the same. And now, explain to
me . . . *Alle länder gute Menschen tragen:* each town has its
good men, yes, but where, Commodore, where are the
Mexicans? I must admit, I said so in a letter to Louis
Napoleon, that in Mexico capable men do not exist . . . and
also, again, that here there are only three classes of men:
the old, who are stubborn and decrepit; the young, who
know nothing; and foreigners, almost all of them mediocre
adventurers . . . with highly honorable exceptions, of
course. . . . There you have General Sterling Price, Governor of Missouri, who lives in a field tent in an orange grove
by the side of the Veracruz railway, and he swears that on
his lands he is going to grow tobacco better than the
Cubans. And we have Brigadier General Daniel Leadbet-
ter of Maine, who is giving so much help for the construction of the railway . . . competent men, Commodore,
West Point graduates . . . ah, and to found Ciudad Carlota,
which will one day rival Richmond. . . ."

"And New Orleans, Sire . . ."

"And New Orleans, Commodore, has sent us Fighting Shelby and his iron brigade . . . or, what are they called? His Iron Cavalry Brigade. . . . I have asked Shelby to write me his reports in verse. Did you know he wrote them that way for confederate headquarters?"

"Yes, your Majesty . . ."

"And of course, you, a world-renowned oceanographer, are also here . . ."

The Emperor passed his binoculars to the oceanographer and meteorologist Matthew Fontaine Maury, and pointed toward the north.

"Look. No, no, a little more to the left. Just a little . . . You see it? You see the shrine of Our Lady of Guadalupe? It has always seemed to me a bit Muscovite. . . . Do you agree? And tell me, what other country in the world can boast of having as director of colonization a man as distinguished as yourself, Commodore Maury?"

"I, Your Majesty, I am only . . ."

". . . the man who brought to Mexico the chinchona tree, and to whom we sufferers of malarial fevers shall one day owe so much? Do you see, Commodore, that little knoll by the side of the shrine? And I should like to acclimatize the alpaca and the llama to Mexico. . . . Do you see it?"

"Yes, Sire . . ."

"It is the Hill of Tepeyac, where the Virgin appeared to the Indian Juan Diego. . . . They tell me, Commodore— what things do not occur to the English!—that they are giving their subjects in their African colonies doses of powdered bark of quinine dissolved in water and gin. . . . They are clever, aren't they, Commodore? They are cunning. And look, below: those silver-colored reflections—you see them? That is Lake Xaltocan."

"Yes, Your Majesty. . . ."

Translated by C. M. Mayo

Day and Night
Mónica Lavín

WHEN THE COUSINS spent their vacations in the house in Acapatzingo, the days had the clarity of a swimming pool and the ferocity of the sun; nights had the impenetrability of obsidian.

To the side of the church, among the sapodilla trees that splattered their black fruits in the garden, the mornings were golden like the beer their parents drank by the side of the pool. The girls would play "school" with the little girls from the town, as there was an empty pigsty that served as a classroom. The girls of the house and the girls of the

MÓNICA LAVÍN (1955–) was born and lives in Mexico City. She has worked as an editor, journalist, radio broadcaster, TV scriptwriter, and professor at the School of Writers of the Mexican Writers Society (SOGEM). She has published several works of fiction, among them the short story collection *Ruby no ha muerto* (1997), which won the Gilberto Owen Prize, and the novel *Café cortado* (2001). She is the editor of *Points of Departure* (2002), an anthology of Mexican fiction in translation, and is on the faculty of the Creative Writing department of the Autonomous University of Mexico City.

town cleaned it and brought in some tables so that the small girls could play student while the big girls gave explanations on the chalkboard they had brought from Mexico City. Getting to know the little girls who lived in Acapatzingo was such fun; it sustained them for the weekends and these long school vacations. Before lunch, they would come back to the house to take a dip. The boys would splash them and make fun of them: What was the matter with the girls? They had a pool to play in. Wasn't it enough to go to school every day? What business did they have with the girls from the town? To the girls, the boys seemed like insensitive dopes. The parents warned, Don't get us wet, while they balanced their sweating beer mugs and speared cubes of abalone with toothpicks.

The boys had tied a rope to a branch of the oak tree that hung over the kidney-shaped pool. They would climb its trunk, hang onto the rope, and swing until they could throw themselves right into the center of the pool. The boldest one would make a somersault in the air. They dared the girls: it was their turn. The girls threw themselves in clumsily. Then they would splash water in each others' faces or play "war." The biggest girls would carry the smallest girls on their shoulders, the boys would do the same, and they would struggle until one of gladiators fell vanquished into the water. Panting, they would go drink cold hibiscus tea. On the terrace, the mothers would serve the girls and boys their lunch, which they ate in their still-wet bathing suits. The girls would then tell the boys about things they could not see because they had been in the pool all day: In Marcela's house they have a she-ass; they have a well to get their water; their mother makes tortillas by hand

and she gave us some; they keep scorpions in a jar; they have a black ribbon over their front door because they have a little brother who died when he was born. The boys would pretend they weren't interested. After lunch they would look for the bow and arrow so they could shoot at the banana tree at the back of the garden and enjoy how that metal tip buried itself in the milky shaft. The girls liked to shoot because of the way the bow tautened so nicely, and when they let it loose, the arrow whistled through the air. Church bells called them to bring flowers to the Virgin. There go the little nuns, the boys would say, because the girls hurried to get dressed, chlorine still in their hair and with their skin streaked by sun and water. Marcela was already at the door: they would go to the ravine to cut fresh flowers. They would go out jubilant in their white or honey-colored sandals, their wet hair pulled back with rubber bands. The boys would wait on the terrace for a while, bored, until they could get permission to once again throw themselves into the pool; the terrace felt wide now that the girls were at mass. How ridiculous: their parents never went.

Entering the dark church, the girls felt part of that multitude of women of all ages. They thought the little bouquets they held in their hands would make them good. Avidly they waited for the moment when the songs they had not yet learned would be sung, so they could come up close to the Virgin's feet and add their flowers to the fragrant mountain. In reverent silence each one searched the Virgin's eyes. They did not even glance at each other; it was as if they did not know each other, as if they belonged to the ritual, as if they had always belonged to the church of their country house.

In the afternoon, the girls would return, taking care not to disturb the grown-ups' siesta, and with the boys (who did not show any pleasure at their return) they would kill what was left of the afternoon with board games or charades to guess movie titles. And so the night arrived with its supper of grilled sandwiches they called flying saucers. Then the boys proposed that they cross the churchyard. The girls wanted to go buy something in the little grocery store that was just on the other side.

"You can go around the church outside it," one girl said.

"That doesn't make sense. Could it be you're scared?" The boys teased.

"Not at all," the girls said and they left behind the bossa nova their parents started listening to after they gave the children coins to buy cookies with pink marshmallows.

They had to climb steps up to the churchyard, which was a vacant lot where they had seen Moors and Christians in ritual battle and heard Margarito the dwarf (who was as small as a doll, but without a big head and arms like the ones in the circus) say in a high voice that he would conquer evil. It looked like a graveyard, flanked by the moonlit ocher church. To the back of the yard they could see the willow, the only tree in that desert. Next to it, though visible from this far corner, were the stairs that went down to the little store. They were going to cross the churchyard at night, but they were not used to doing it; their hearts were pounding fast and their mouths went dry. This darkness could be the territory of La Llorona, the weeping ghostwoman. It did not look at all the way it had a few hours ago when they were saying the rosary or swinging on the rope. No one wanted to go first or be last. For unbearable minutes it seemed it was one or the other; for this reason the smallest ones did not have to participate in the coin toss to decide the order.

After an eternity of tripping over dark, dry ground, once on the other side, their fear turned to pride, which came out as nervous laughter. Each one thought it was the last time they would do that. The return would be at a full run and around the wall. Someone proposed collecting money to a buy a pack of cigarettes. And, they added, some Chiclets to hide the smell. The man in the grocery store gave them matches; it didn't bother him to be selling cigarettes to kids. Not wanting to be seen, they went around the corner of the wall, away from the man. The oldest boy lit the first cigarette. He took several puffs until the tip glowed red in the dark. He passed it to the oldest girl. She coughed a bit. She took a puff and let out a plume of smoke. She passed the cigarette, which made all of them cough and laugh and want it to go around again so they could take another puff. They lit the next cigarette with the stub of the last, the way they'd seen their parents do. And when they were finished, they weren't sure what to do with the rest of the pack; it seemed to them to have been enough. Already some of them were dizzy and their mouths had a disagreeable taste. They handed around the cinnamon Chiclets and walked slowly and quietly back to the house to end the day with some TV, all of them sprawled on the mattress in the master bedroom, complaining and laughing, until sleep overcame them.

On the Saturday of their April vacation that their cousin Elena arrived with her mother to spend the day, the boys and girls tried to keep to their routines and schedules.

Elena was already thirteen years old; she refused to play "school" with the neighbor girls. Neither did she want to throw herself from the rope into the freezing-cold pool. With her long blond braid that divided her back in two and wearing her navy-blue bikini, she lay down on one of the chaises.

The girls returned quickly from classes in the pigsty and the boys stopped playing Tarzan, so as to not splash their cousin's svelte body. They ate their snacks around Elena, who joined them so she could reach for a jicama. With their legs and torsos so close, the boys and the girls could see that her calves were smooth. Elena shaved them. At once, the girls wanted to get rid of the fuzz on their own legs; the boys, to lean into those bronzing thighs.

They ate with less commotion and without showing each other their food. Elena spoke little. Slightly bored, she asked if they would spend all of their vacations in this place.

The girls and boys turned back to their plates of lentils, feeling the coming days as a jumbled-up burden. Bells in the distance enlivened the girls. They invited Elena. She said she only went to mass on Sundays. This pleased the boys, as they assumed she would do archery or play with the BB gun, but Elena lay down with a magazine in the living room, where it was cooler. From the terrace, the boys looked at her from time to time without being able to tear themselves away.

The girls tossed flowers at the appointed hour, feeling a certain haste to return and less devotion to the porcelain statue's saintly eyes. They asked if Elena wanted to go to the churchyard when it got dark. The boys had already proposed it to her. She liked the idea of getting out of the house, and while they were walking, now that the sun had gone down, she seemed more agreeable. The boys and girls were thrilled that she would venture to cross the church-yard and not think they were stupid.

Are there any men around? she asked them in the dark-ness when they were deciding the order. They had thought of La Llorona and other varmints. Men did not cross the churchyard at night.

"Not even drunks?" she asked.

They tossed the coin. It was Elena who had to go first. The oldest boy exchanged places with her. She would be second. The others watched this, perplexed; he had never done anything like that before. When they all reached the other side of the barren churchyard, Elena already had the pack in her hands. She gave a cigarette to each one. This time they did not bother to stay out of the shop owner's sight. They smoked there beneath the willow, with their wisps of smoke challenging the churchyard's black empti-ness, which they had mastered. Elena explained that in order to smoke properly, you had to inhale, and she gave a demonstration. She took a puff on the cigarette and opened her empty mouth, so they could imagine the smoke swirling around in her lungs. Then she made two smoke rings, which they watched in amazement. They tried to do it but it made them dizzy; no one thought of those handy cinnamon Chiclets.

They returned to the house with a light step and Elena in the center because she knew how to smoke and had not coughed and walked upright as if the smoke that had made arabesques in her lungs had given her a certain pride. They forgot the TV and went into the children's room, the one with the foldout beds, which opened onto the terrace. In the narrow space between the beds they were sitting on, they played spin the bottle. Yes, kisses and slaps and then passing the lighted match: whoever dropped it had to answer a rude question. And then they couldn't think of anything to do until someone switched off the light, and the oldest boy turned on the lantern and asked the women to do a show for the boys. All together, almost falling over each other, the boys climbed up onto the high bed. And the girls thought of a dance. The oldest boy held the lantern like a spotlight on each girl and Elena lifted her leg as if she were dancing a cancan. Then they traded places, and the boys made a pyramid, one on top of the other, but they all fell down when one of the girls shined the lantern in their eyes. Then the boys asked Elena to do a show by herself. The girls also said yes and they climbed onto the other bed, the one without the lantern, for the boys had taken possession of it. Elena went to the corner by the door so that everybody could see her, and she began to sway like a woman, her hips one way, then the other, her waist making circles. She pretended to take off her shoes and pantyhose, though she wasn't wearing any, and she turned her back to the whistles of the boys and the girls who were pretending to be customers in a cabaret. And she pretended to be taking off her dress and unbuttoning her bra and tossing it off, though she still had on her red striped T-shirt and khaki shorts, until the oldest boy dared to say: Lift up your shirt. And with their silence, all agreed. And he shined the light on her waist as Elena held the edge of her T-shirt and slowly raised it to show her stomach and then, like a surprising landscape, her budding breasts. They did not whistle; they did not even applaud. The oldest boy shut off the lantern, and it was a good thing Elena's mother knocked on the door to say they were leaving.

The next morning they sunned themselves on the chaises and went in the pool. The girls did not answer when Marcela came to knock on the door for class, nor did the boys pay any attention to the rope that hung there, useless. The girls did not respond to the church bells or the women's footsteps as they went to the ravine to gather flowers. The arrow did not sing through the air, nor wound the plant. They laughed less and played little. They were merely waiting for the night, which they had already confused with the day.

Translated by C. M. Mayo

Huaquechula

Pedro Ángel Palou

YOU RING THE DOORBELL cautiously, or worse yet, fearfully. As if you were afraid of being a nuisance, knowing that even your presence is a fly in the soup of Adela's weekends. She opens the door and gives you a frigid, dutiful kiss, the usual Saturday kiss, a kiss so cold that your cheek feels no desire but accepts it as the only possible contact. The girls are ready, all dressed up, with their hair pulled back coquettishly at the nape. They smell nice, which is nothing new. They shout *Papá* and run up to you for a hug. You lift them as if they weighed almost nothing and you whirl them through the air like little airplanes.

PEDRO ÁNGEL PALOU (1966–) was born in Puebla. He is the author of more than fifteen books, among them the novels *En la alcoba de un mundo* (1992), *Memoria de los días* (1996), *Demasiadas vidas* (2002), and *Malheridos* (2003), as well as the story collection *Amores enormes* (1991), which won the Jorge Ibargüengoitia Prize. His book *La casa del silencio* (1998) won the Francisco Xavier Clavigero National Prize for History. He has worked as a professor, publisher, and cultural agent, and currently is the Minister of Culture for his native state.

You're going to mess up their hair, you fear Adela will say, but she doesn't.

"Say goodbye to your mother," you tell them and they grudgingly disentangle themselves from you and obey. You take them by the hand and go down the stairs.

Before you all get into the car, a window opens from above and you hear her shout:

"Don't arrive late at night, no later than eight, do you hear me?"

You nod but don't answer her. When you pull the car out, you feel as if the escaping exhaust were freeing you, although you don't know from what.

"Where are we going today?" asks your youngest daughter, the one you know least. Which side of the bed does she sleep on, for example?

The other one, Sara, echoes her:

"*Sí, Papá*, where?"

"We're going to the zoo," the two of them say.

You can't imagine spending another Saturday watching rude baboons displaying their pink buttocks and spitting through the bars. You feel badly about using your day with them to do work, but even so, you suggest:

"Why don't we go to Huaquechula?"

"What's that?" asks Regina, the younger girl.

You explain to them and both seem enthusiastic about going to a village and seeing altars to the dead, although they can't imagine what it's really about. But when you arrive, they realize.

"Are you going to take pictures?" they ask as you arrange your camera, the lenses, and the rolls of film in the case.

"It's the only thing I know how to do, girls."

"But what about us?"

"Wouldn't you like me to take your picture next to the altars?"

They tell you *all right* with resignation: they'd forbidden you to take photos of animals during your weekends together at the zoo. In fact, they'd forbidden you to take any photos, exasperated about all the time you dedicate to framing the shot, focusing, adjusting the light, the ideal film for this climate, and an endless number of etceteras.

Isabel had also told you, not without sarcasm, do you remember? *You no longer take photos for* National Geographic, *Eduardo, why such trouble for a lousy second-rate newspaper that doesn't even pay you?*

Three months, you repeat to yourself, the romance with Isabel lasted three months, ninety-two days, and the nights that accompanied them. And then, *Fuck off. This isn't working, Eduardo, your presence bothers me. I can't stand how you take up space.* It wasn't desire, it wasn't tenderness. Sooner or later, it will be part of the past; it wasn't solitude or sadness, you tell yourself. You felt clumsy, like a drunk clinging to a wall before he falls unavoidably into a puddle. No, no, it wasn't the silence, or the love, you repeat to yourself. Perhaps it wasn't even her face, or her body, or her company, or her words. The words of lovers when they separate are terrible, although they're tinged with a false sense of security or happiness. Good-bye. *They say that farewells aren't sad,* you hum to yourself, *tell whoever told you,* cielito lindo, *to say farewell.*

There was no way of approaching Adela to tell her it was over with Isabel, ask her to again make a place for you in her life. Or at least in your apartment. No, you'd arrange things by yourself, you thought. But how long would that take? A year of going to pick up the girls, ringing the damned doorbell, and then getting bored and boring them all day just to end up in a cantina, invariably weeping at a table in the back.

"Shall we go in?" you ask Sara as you point to one of the first open houses. In Huaquechula all the altars are white, with towers consisting of many stories filled with prints of angels and cherubim in pastel colors. The ceiling of each story has mirrors that reflect the photos of the deceased to whom the altar is dedicated; the mirrors' purpose is to prevent the dead person's presence from dissolving, to keep the spirit inside the house with his or her loved ones on holy days. You ask permission to take photographs and they tell you *yes*, courteously. You ask an old woman whom the altar is dedicated to.

"My dead husband."

"When did he die?" you inquire, imprudently.

"Almost a month ago, and I couldn't find anyone to build me the altar, everyone was too busy."

You tell her you're sorry, that it must be hard to be here tending to her husband's return.

"He was a drunk, so we filled it with bottles of tequila and his cigarettes. Those were the things he liked."

As the two of you speak, you take a few photos; you linger on one shot, in particular, in which you can see the image of the photo reflected by the mirror on the second story. You've always thought that in Huaquechula the altars look like enormous white cakes. The woman explains to you that they only put up the altar to the dead person the first year and then it's common to open the house and offer food to all the visitors, even if they're strangers, so they can keep the family company in its grief.

The girls are now sitting down, eating tamales and drinking *atole*, and a woman is speaking kindly to them. You pause before taking the photo.

"What did he die of?" you ask boldly, intrusively, again.

"They ran him over, can you believe it? After he endured eighty-six years and who knows how many problems in his life, they crush him with a truck. He was very drunk, as usual. It makes me so mad, he left me all alone."

"But what about your children, your grandchildren?" you ask, trying to console her.

"It's not the same, young man. To be without a husband isn't healthy; who's going to caress you at night?"

You remember the cold sheets, returning to a house you thought was temporary, that's become just a place to sleep, a place where you don't want to return each night. She's right, you tell yourself. You accept something to drink and sit down. The people in Huaquechula withdraw all their savings so they can invite everyone else to share their mourning. The more company, the better.

You say good-bye to each other and the old woman offers some sugar skulls to the girls, writing their names on them—Sara, Regina—and gives them each a kiss.

"*Papá*, that smell makes me dizzy," Regina tells you.

"*Sí, Papá*, why is there so much smoke?"

You explain but don't convince either them or yourself. Actually, the copal and the incense *do* make one dizzy— the dozens of lit candles, the prayers, the faith. It's good to have faith in something, Adela would have said, knowing that you never could believe in anything. Out of skepticism or insensitivity?

This year there are twelve altars, which means that twelve people have died. One per month, you tell yourself, as you photograph them all. One by one, the same ritual, the same questions. There isn't a mournful air in any of them. Nobody weeps. You wished you had their resignation, their capacity for acceptance. One is for a two-year-old boy. This makes an impression on Sara and her eyes fill with tears.

"Poor thing, what happened to him?" she asks as you're leaving. You shrug your shoulders. You don't know and don't want to know. Or do you? For them, the altar is just that, a form of presenting themselves to the dead; for you, it's a visual pretext. Meanwhile, the better the photos turn out, the more satisfied you'll be, they'll select more of them to illustrate the newspaper and your name will appear beneath them. And the mourning? In reality, that was what Sara was asking you, where was the mourning? But that's something you can't answer, something you yourself have fought to silence until you've stopped feeling. All this goes through your head at the last altar, number twelve. It's for a forty-year-old woman who died of cancer, according to her husband; he keeps vigil as he tends to her altar. You contemplate the photo. She was beautiful. It seems curious that this one doesn't have a mirror on it. You dare to ask the cause of death; it's so strange, you tell him, that they haven't attached any mirrors.

"To leave her in peace. I set up the altar for my mother, who asked me to do it, but I refused to put in her mirror. I didn't want her spirit to go wandering around here. I already gave her enough trouble while she was alive. I told her, it's to let her rest in peace."

And it occurs to you now, just today, when you were thinking of telling Adela to forgive you, that it had been a long time since the thing with Isabel ended. Let me love you again, you'd planned to tell her, if not for you—the blackmail would continue—then for the girls. Maybe that man was right and it wouldn't be fair for you to arrive now and ruin her life.

You leave there bewildered, but not from the incense or the wax of so many lit candles. Besides, you've taken more than three hundred photos. But the whole atmosphere has disturbed you. You begin thinking about Isabel. What made you decide? One day, not letting any more time pass, you spoke with Adela. She'd already known, she told you, but she thought it wasn't serious, that it was only an adventure. *How stupid of me, really, to think that you'd want to fall in love!* she told you, before asking you to leave as soon as you could, without saying good-bye to the girls; eventually she'd explain it to them. And she didn't let you see them for two months, until all the arrangements were made for the divorce and then, one day, she imposed her conditions. It was more humiliating when she said *you have the right to see the girls on Saturdays* than when she didn't let you see them at all. Besides, that didn't really bother you then, you were living with Isabel, which means that you and Isabel were fucking like animals all over the apartment, sleeping naked, and waking up very late to sniff each other out and start all over again.

Until she decided to end what for her, you tell yourself, must have been an adventure.

You remember the scene perfectly, you haven't done anything but repeat it these past months:

"You don't understand, isn't that true, Eduardo? My life has been full of people who learned to love me and who made me afraid to love them back. I loved you intensely for a while, I didn't feel I was losing much—the idea of getting half an ass like a piece in a lousy puzzle terrifies some people, it makes them greedy for more—then you began to bother me, to invade my space."

"I gave you everything, Isabel."

"The problem is the word *everything*. I didn't want to give you everything, although at times it may have seemed that way and even *we* believed the lie for a couple of months. I didn't want you to give me everything, either; the responsibility of that burden seems obscene to me."

"How did I blow it?" you hear yourself asking Isabel. Now that you think about it, you feel naive, an incredible imbecile, for using that phrase.

"No, Eduardo, I'm not reproaching you in any way, but how can I live with an extra limb? It doesn't do it for me—it's not a luxury I can afford. I should have been a man. Surely then you'd understand me."

You think about all this as you leave the altar, until Regina tells you that Adela's boyfriend has just passed by.

"What do you mean, your mother's 'boyfriend'?"

"Hasn't she told you? He's a really nice guy," Regina says.

"He's stuck up, it's just that he brings you a lot of gifts, but I hate him," Sara contradicts her and the two of them begin quarreling about a guy you don't know and whom the girls think they've seen in Huaquechula.

"And what's his name?"

"Baraquiel."

You don't imagine archangels; you don't have the brains to enter the celestial court he must belong to. You only associate him, right away, with Lucifer. It seems ridiculous, but you think it: *fallen angel*. It makes you laugh, but it also enrages you.

"And what does he do?"

"He's my mother's boyfriend," Regina says.

"That's not a profession."

There's no point in arguing. They climb into the car as if something had broken. You're all silent, the girls know that they've broken something deep inside you, or they sense it, and don't say anything. Maybe for that reason the trip seems long. Or the return, as you'd prefer to call it. You eat in a restaurant where they serve trout; it's right next to a fish farm where the girls toss the fish food that smells horrible, or so it seems to you. One of those trout was your meal, you think, as you watch them swim against the current and it begins to rain.

You all run to the car, the girls laughing and getting wet. You immediately think about Adela, about what she'll say when she first sees them. The entire highway is a long lament from heaven, you tell yourself, but the metaphor doesn't please you.

You ring the doorbell; this time the girls press it again, rap their knuckles on the door, and gently kick it with their tennis shoes.

When Adela opens the door, they overwhelm her and run in, shouting.

"It's time for their favorite program," Adela explains

and smiles at you. For the first time in a year she smiles at you, or is it a grimace? Maybe she can't hide her happiness at being with a man again, you think.

"Are you getting married?" you ask her, point-blank.

"Where does that come from?"

"Just answer me, are you getting married?"

"In the first place, it's none of your business, and in the second, what did those two tell you?"

"It's nothing, they told me you had a boyfriend, that he brought them presents, that he was a cool guy, and who knows how many other things."

"Well, yes, maybe I *am* getting married. And now's a good time for you to leave, don't you think?"

You keep quiet. There's a long silence. You both glare, as if you were going to attack each other, to wage the final battle, the definitive one. Two beasts, that's what you think, we're two beasts.

"Or do you have something to tell me?"

You shake your head and leave, without saying good-bye, better to leave her in peace, like the man with the altar said. The rest of the night passes quickly, two, maybe three hours spent developing and printing the contact sheets in the darkroom of your apartment. Demanding work that allows you to forget. Sprinkled with lots of tequila, of course, like they do for all the dead, so they'll return, although for you no return is possible.

At the end of the day's work, annoyed with yourself for your meticulousness, you go to bed, but it's as if an enormous boulder were falling on the mattress. You turn off the light, hoping that your next dream—because you always dream—is pleasant and refreshing. You've sealed the envelope, also meticulously, that contains the photos of Huaquechula to be picked up by messenger in the morning; this time, you're not allowing yourself the luxury of remaining blue. There's no mirror, especially this time, for the spirit—if it even exists—to leave the body, to float away, and go where it pleases. Before closing your eyes, you're assaulted by worry: what demons will you stir up next Saturday with the girls? And the next one after that? Until what point? Hopefully they'll reach eighteen soon, you tell yourself, and they themselves will send you far away, like their mother did. Will you be jealous of their boyfriends? You see Regina on top of a headstone making love with a boy in a leather jacket and it disgusts you. You drink a glass of water, but it's hard to swallow, as if a fine, invisible knot were choking you. Even so, you feel no pain, no sorrow.

Before you drop off to sleep, you think about Adela for the last time; you contemplate her face, clearly defined but in black and white, as if you were seeing her in an old photograph. She smiles at you, Eduardo, for the first time in a year, she smiles at you, or is it a grimace?

Translated by Daniel Shapiro

Aunt Elena

Ángeles Mastretta

ARROYO ZARCO PLANTATION was a large strip of fertile land in the mountains north of Puebla. In 1910 its owners planted coffee and sugarcane, corn, beans, and other vegetables. The landscape was green year-round. It rained while the sun shone, while it didn't shine, and beneath the moon. The rain seemed so natural that no one thought twice about putting on a raincoat to go out for a walk.

Aunt Elena lived but a short time in this dampness. For one thing, there were no schools nearby, so her parents sent her to the Sacred Heart high school in Mexico City. She was three hundred kilometers away there—twenty

ÁNGELES MASTRETTA (1949–) was born in the state of Puebla and moved to Mexico City in 1971. One of Mexico's leading feminist journalists and writers, she has published in major Mexican newspapers such as *Excelsior* and *Unomásuno*, and magazines including *Nexos* and *Ovaciones*. Among her novels are *Mexican Bolero* (1985) and *Lovesick* (1997), which won the prestigious Rómulo Gallegos Prize. Her most recent novel is *El cielo de Los Leones* (2003). This story is taken from *Women with Big Eyes* (2003), her collection of thirty-nine fictional portraits of Mexican women, all purportedly the narrator's aunts.

hours by train, with a snack and a night's sleep in the city of Puebla, and a breakfast already governed by the nostalgia that ten months spent far from her mother's extravagant cooking and close to French and the caravans of barren nuns would provoke. Later, when she had completed her studies with honors in arithmetic, grammar, history, geography, piano, needlework, French, and calligraphy, and had returned to the country and the happy anxiety of living there, she had to leave again, because the Revolution came.

When the usurpers entered the plantation to take possession of its fields and waters, Aunt Elena's father put up no resistance. He handed over the house, the patio, the chapel, and the furniture with the same show of courtesy that had always distinguished him from the other plantation owners. His wife showed the soldiers the way to the kitchen, and he took out the titles that evinced his ownership of the plantation, and delivered them to the leader of the rebellion in the state.

Then he moved his family to Teziutlán, settled comfortably in a carriage and practically smiling.

They had always been famous for being half crazy, so when they showed up in town whole and at peace, the other landowners were sure that Ramos Lanz had something to do with the rebels. It could not be pure coincidence that they hadn't burned down his house, or that his daughters didn't seem terrorized, or that his wife was not in tears.

The Ramoses were viewed badly when they walked around town, talkative and happy as though nothing bad had happened to them. The father's demeanor was so steady and gentle that none of the family saw fit to upset him. After all, if he smiled it was merely because the next day and the next decade there would be food on the table and crinolines beneath the silk skirts. It was because no one would be left without hair combs, or without lockets, or clasps, or diamond earrings, or without port to drink.

They saw him worried only one afternoon. He passed several hours at the desk in the house in Teziutlán, drawing something that looked like a map, which he could not leave alone. He threw sheet after sheet into the wastebasket, feeling as useless as one who tries to remember a route to treasures buried centuries earlier.

Aunt Elena watched him from an armchair without saying a word, without paying attention to anything but his actions. Suddenly she saw him relax and heard him speak to himself in a whisper, but not so softly that she missed his euphoria. He folded his paper in quarters and threw it into a bag.

"Is it suppertime yet?" he asked, looking at her for the first time, without revealing anything or speaking of what had kept him occupied all afternoon.

"I'll go see," she said, and she went to the kitchen, making up her mind about something. When she returned, her father was asleep in a very high-backed armchair. She slowly drew near and went to the wastebasket to salvage a few of the pieces of paper he had thrown away. She put them inside a book and then woke him to tell him supper was ready.

Everything was huge in the Ramos house. Even in these times of scarcity, Aunt Elena's mother got herself organized to make seven-course meals and dinner for at least five people. That night there was mushroom soup, *torta de masa*, pepper strips with tomatoes, and refried beans. The menu ended with chocolate water and shiny sugared breads that Aunt Elena never saw again until after the Revolution. With all this in their stomachs, the family went to sleep and to grow fat without a single regret.

Of the eight daughters Señora Ramos had borne, five had died of illnesses such as smallpox, whooping cough, and asthma, so the three who lived grew up overfed. According to popular belief, it was the good and plentiful food that helped them survive. But that night Aunt Elena's father surprised his family by not being very hungry.

"Eat, little bird, you're going to get sick," Doña Otilia begged her husband, a man of one hundred eighty centimeters from his feet to the tip of his head and ninety kilos who guarded her soul.

Elena asked for permission to leave the table before finishing the last bite of her sugared bread and went to shut herself up in the guest room with a candle. There she put together the pieces of paper and read the green ink in which her father wrote: the map had a footpath, which arrived at the plantation from somewhere behind the house and led directly to the underground room they had constructed near the kitchen.

The wines! The only regret her father had since the usurpers took Arroyo Zarco was the loss of his wines, his collection of bottles with labels in many languages, full of a beverage that she had sipped from the adults' cups since she was a small child. Her father, that steady and moderate man, could he be capable of returning to the plantation for his wines? Was it for that she had heard him at midday asking Cirilo for a wagon with a horse and straw?

Aunt Elena grabbed a shawl and flew down the stairs. In the dining room, her father was still looking for excuses to explain to his wife the grave sin of not being hungry.

"It's not contempt, my love. I know all the trouble it takes you to prepare each meal so that we don't miss the previous one. But tonight I have something to take care of and I don't want to have a heavy stomach."

At the moment she heard her father say "tonight," Aunt Elena ran out to the patio in search of the carriage. The servant Cirilo had hooked it up to a horse and was watching in silence. Why hadn't Cirilo gone to fight in the Revolution? Why was he standing here silently, next to the horse, in the same soliloquy as always? Aunt Elena crept on tiptoe and climbed into the back of the carriage. After a short while, she heard her father's voice.

"Did you find good straw?" he asked the servant.

"Yes, master. Would you like to see it?"

Aunt Elena thought that her father had nodded, because she heard him move near the back of the carriage and lift a corner of the straw sleeping mat. She felt her father's hand move within three hand lengths of her body:

"The straw is very good," he said, moving away.

Then Aunt Elena regained her soul and loosened the stiffness in her neck.

"You are not coming, Cirilo," said Señor Ramos. "This is a folly of my body that, if it costs anyone, I want to cost only me. If I don't return, tell my wife that all the meals she made in my life were delicious, and tell my daughter

Elena that I didn't seek her out to give her a kiss, because I want to keep owing it to her."

"Godspeed," Cirilo told him.

The carriage began to move slowly; slowly it left the town behind in darkness and moved along a road that must have been as straight as Aunt Elena imagined it when she saw it painted with a single line. There was no room on either side of the carriage, so the horse could not run the way it did when she drove it on a wide road.

It took them more than an hour to arrive, but because she fell asleep it seemed like a short time to Aunt Elena. She awoke as the carriage almost stopped moving, and she heard nothing in the air but the "Sss-sss" with which her father calmed the horse. She lifted her head to see where they were, and saw before her the back of the enormous house she had loved her whole life. Her father stopped the carriage and got down. She saw him tremble below the half-moon. Apparently no one was guarding the place. Her father walked to a door and opened it with a huge key. Then he disappeared. Aunt Elena got out from under the straw and followed him into the wine cellar, which was illuminated by a newly lit lantern.

"Can I help you?" she asked him in her hoarse voice. Her face was sleepy and her hair full of straw fibers.

She would never forget the horror she saw in her father's eyes. For the first time in her life she felt afraid, despite having him close by.

"I like port too," she said, controlling her own shaking. She picked up two bottles and went to put them in the straw of the carriage. Upon returning, she passed her father, who was carrying four others. They came and went like this in silence, until the carriage was full and there wasn't room in it for even one of those ports she had learned to drink on the knees of that man so prudent and faithful to his habits, who surprised her that night with his craziness.

He took two more bottles to pay his toll, and put them between his legs. Then he harnessed the horse to the carriage and made his way toward the narrow hidden road by which they had arrived. They would be hours in returning, but it was a miracle that they were about to leave without anyone's having seen them. Not one of the peasants who occupied Arroyo Zarco watched over the back of the plantation.

"Could they all have gone?" Aunt Elena asked her father, and jumped from the carriage without giving him time to grab her. She ran to the house, pressed herself against the darkness of a wall, and walked close to it until she turned the corner. Finally she bumped against a bench that once guarded the main door. There was no light in all that darkness. Not a voice, or a screech, or footsteps, or a single open window.

"There's no one here!" screamed Aunt Elena. "There's no one here!" she repeated balling her hands into fists and jumping up and down.

They returned via the bog road. Aunt Elena hummed "An Old Love" with the nostalgia of an old lady. At eighteen, the loves of a day before are already old. And so many things had happened to her that night that suddenly she felt in her loves a hole impossible to mend. Who would believe her adventure? Her small-town boyfriend, not a word.

"Elena, for God's sake, stop talking nonsense," he told her, alarmed, when he heard her tale. "These are not times for fantasy. I know it hurts you to have left the plantation, but don't ruin your father's good name telling tales that make him look like an irresponsible drunkard."

But she had already lost her father, beneath the merciless moon of the previous night, and she didn't even try to convince her boyfriend. A week later, she climbed aboard the train car into which her mother was able to fit everything from the Louis XV parlor to ten hens, two roosters, and a cow with her bull calf. Aunt Elena carried with her no more baggage than the future and the early certainty that the most honorable of men had a screw loose.

Translated by Amy Schildhouse Greenberg

Banquets
Raúl Mejía

We do not eat to nourish ourselves. Humans, at least, do not. If we did, we would simply eat. But human beings have made eating a ceremony, a rite so sacred that it could be a mass. The mass itself, in ancient days, was a gastronomic ceremony— poor, austere, but utterly gastronomic.

—José Luis Muñoz

IT WAS ALWAYS WITH A BIT of a sneer that people in my neighborhood used the word "banquet." We knew that we would never attend the kind of feast we saw in the movies. We used the word "banquet" for Rosita's enchiladas, rich with grease, onions, and cheese. Or for those *gorditas* of Doña Paula—even now I recall them, full of potatoes and dripping with sausage grease, or with beans simmered with bacon strips. That was a banquet. Although

---

RAÚL MEJÍA (1956–) lives in Morelia, Michoacán, where he is a professor of literature and the host of a radio program. He is the author of several collections of short stories, including *Triques* (1988), *En la línea* (1992), and *Banquetes* (1995). In 1993 he was awarded the Michoacán State Prize for the Short Story. His most recent books are *Estaciones de paso* (2004) and *Índice de filas y fobias* (2005), both of literary prose.

of course the word also had overtones of something extra-ordinary. Maybe a first Communion party with hot choco-late and cake with sickly-sweet frosting. Not especially tasty, or nutritious, or even exotic, just not ordinary. A ban-quet meant new clothes: a dress whiter than white, pants so new they were stiff, hair slicked back. A banquet was an event. It didn't even have to be associated with food, despite the long white tablecloths. It was a chance to cut loose in somebody else's house. Always of course with some party—I mean banquet—as a pretext.

It was a banquet when our parents took my brothers and me—whenever they had a bit left over after payday—to the Café Morelos for chilies (pasillas, I mean, not poblanos) coated in beaten egg and stuffed with cheese or tuna. It was a banquet to go to El Paraíso afterward for the dessert we'd been anticipating for fifteen days. Or for sixty. The banana split that flirted with people who couldn't afford it via photos in the front window.

Those were the banquets of a childhood spent among tough folk. Our neighbors were the hookers and queers who lived in apartments like ours, although we were the only ones who called them apartments. Anybody else would've called it a slum. Pimps operated less than two hundred yards from our house. People said that they were the fathers of two or three of my friends. The truth of the matter was that my friends themselves didn't know who their fathers were. Not even their own mothers could've told them who had launched them into slum life. They were bastards and they knew it. And nobody cared.

Living a few yards from the red-light district let me view a lot of fights, stuff that either ended with police sweeps or with Saturday morning corpses. Hookers' quarrels. Guys rolling drunks who were passed out in the street. I got kicked out of bars for ignoring the sign that every whorehouse displayed: No Minors, Nobody in Uniform, No Soliciting. But I did manage to satisfy my curiosity. It was a shadowy atmosphere—some of the women kept themselves up, others were utterly gross, and all were sad. Whoever paid for a ticket could squeeze their buttocks and dance "six-pack style." That's what they called it, the older guys. And they knew what they were talking about.

Walking home my friends and I would talk about the weird stuff we'd seen, imagining what it would be like to get all messy behind those curtains that separated the dancing from "the other stuff." Our nightlife didn't prevent us, of course, from going to Sunday mass at seven in the morning.

And it was at mass that I once again heard the word "banquet." I studied, after all, with nuns. Mass was part of my upbringing. We learned the creed and the Litanies by heart. So what if we were hanging out in whorehouses by age nine?

But there was one small hitch in my development as a Catholic. I was the only one of the guys who couldn't take mass. Alejandro and Pepe and Tony, Snot Locker and The Violin—everybody but me had been confirmed by age seven. Just like you were supposed to do in our neighborhood. My brother and I were the only ones who couldn't take Communion. So when the priest opened mass— "Welcome to the Lord's banquet," and then raised the Host—I knew I was missing something cool. I studied the other guys' faces; they were contrite, devout.

Something divine had to be going on here. The minute the priest pronounced the words "The Body of Christ," they opened their mouths beatifically—Jano and Littleboy, Piggy and Güicho, guys who only knew how to talk trash. I was impressed. I stood there envying the grace that filled those foul little mouths.

It was useless to beg my parents. The fact that my brother and I were now eleven and nine seemed to create, in my mother and father, not a bit of guilt. They just kept saying "later." Later they would make us regular Catholics.

Only the last part of the mass seemed to me to be, strictly speaking, a banquet. The part where they gave out the Host. When my friends came back to the pew they had the faces of cherubs. They looked like they'd sampled a bit of grace in the form of Christ's body. The banquet part was when the priest put a tasty scrap of holy flour in your mouth. You chewed it as slowly as if it were one of Doña Paula's gorditas. The chalice the priest lifted with closed eyes had to contain some kind of fruit-flavored wine. That was the banquet. Forget the rites and double-talk that came with it. I knew nothing about that part. But should I keep missing out just because my parents were lazy?

So one day when the biggest lowlife of all came back to the pew—the worst wise guy in the gang—I asked him: What happens when somebody takes Communion without having been through catechism? Alejandro opened his eyes with a dreamy look. There he knelt with his sins forgiven, making a strange face. As if he were choking down something bitter. He motioned for me to wait.

What happens if I ask for a Host? I insisted. He stood up. Out of the corner of his mouth he asked if I'd been confessed. No, I said, but Mother Altagracia says that people can confess without having received first Communion.

What we can't do is take the Host. Then no, he snapped, sitting down in the pew. You can't. It would be a mortal sin. Mortal? I was feeling real pain. Mortal, he cut me off. OK, what does the Body of Christ taste like? I wanted to know. I don't know, he confessed. It sticks in your throat. It's real hard to swallow. Was that how come you made a face when I wondered what would happen if I asked for one? Uh-huh.

Time went by. I kept going to seven o'clock Sunday mass, eyeing the confessional and envying guys who could say what their sins were. One time I even got in line to do it. I listened carefully to hear what the right words were. But it was hard. Everything was in whispers. But there I was in line, and the priest called me forward. I knelt before him.

Ave María Purísima, he said. I beg your pardon, I said, getting scared. Ave María Purísima, he repeated, bored. I can barely hear you, father. Could you speak a little louder? I said Ave María Purísima, my son! Do I tell you my sins now, father?

Maybe it was because he was bored. Anyhow he overlooked my not knowing how to respond. Sure, he told me, go ahead. I always had my sins memorized. I even had a few invented. The most daring was the one about having seen Laurita Escamilla naked in the bathroom. In truth I was ten centimeters too short to look through the peephole Piggy had cut in the bathroom door to spy on his cousin. Anyway, I finished. And the priest gave me a kindly penitence. Three Our Fathers. He blessed me and I walked away absolutely beatific. Well, almost.

Acting like I knew what I was doing, I walked up with

my arms over my chest like a little lamb. Ready to hear the mystery of mass and help myself to this illegal banquet. The closer I got, the more uneasy I felt. Purified of their sneaky visits to whorehouses, my friends awaited the Eucharist, the thing that let them visit whorehouses all week long. The acolyte rang the bell. The incense made everything feel divine. This was the moment. Everything was decided. I was invited to the banquet. No matter what the cost. Those who are going to take Communion—the priest intoned—please stand in line.

Everybody did. I waited for the right moment when I could avoid explaining what I was doing here among the elect, waiting to receive the lamb of God. I stood at the end of the line. But once again I didn't know the protocol. Should I say something specific? How could I tell? Everybody was talking as quietly as they could. I walked up as if approaching a firing squad. The priest eyed me, indifferent. The Body of Christ, he said. I opened my mouth and closed my eyes. The Body of Christ, he repeated.

At that moment I understood that the Lord's ways were not just mysterious; they were every bit as demanding as any university class. How come you had to study so hard just to swallow a bit of blessed bread? And yet, the Holy Spirit lit up my darkness. Mouth still open, ready to receive the Host, I mumbled something like "agarfasla," and it had the right effect. The Host sat on my tongue. I shifted it to the place in my mouth appropriate for such a sublime morsel, and waited for something transcendental to happen. Maybe some unknown happiness, some quintessential wisdom, something out of this world anyway. But no. Nothing.

I walked off acting melancholy, head down, waiting for something supernatural to occur. Just the way I had seen other guys fake it. There sat Alejandro making his horrible, post-wafer faces. He opened his eyes wide, unable to believe what he saw when I knelt beside him, already suffering what I was sure was the beginning of divine punishment: the Host wouldn't come unstuck from the roof of my mouth. I had never seen anybody simply dislodge the thing with a twist of the tongue and savor it. Alejandro's efforts, for example, left him making comic faces. Maybe what I was about to do had never occurred to him. Did you really have to leave that scrap of flour stuck where it was? It didn't seem fair. Although, of course, the Church's ritual wasn't fair. I closed my eyes tight, ready to see in the shadows the hungry jaws of purgatory swing wide to receive me. I bit the Host and eased my eyes open, ready to see my surroundings vanished. But there sat Alejandro, eyes wide with disbelief.

What'd you do? he asked sternly. I took Communion, dipshit. If you haven't made first Communion, you're going straight to hell. At least you didn't bite the Host, did you? Yes, I bit the Host because it stuck to the roof of my mouth. It didn't taste like much of anything anyway. Biting the Host is a mortal sin, he whispered, and now you're really damned.

Alejandro never knew the impact his words had on me. What I had done weighed on me for years. Even in 1968 when my folks decided to take the big step and send their three sons to receive first Communion, I kept thinking I was a heretic. I never told anybody what I had done. Not till now, not till now.

And so we kept on living in La Soterraña barrio—kids wide-eyed at red-light-district scenes. I even got to where I could slip into Mary's Bar and sneak a dance with one of the employees. All of us did that, one by one, before we turned fourteen. Before long the oldest of us, Bug Eyes—at fifteen he was able to boast the shadow of a mustache—was getting into the Río Rosa and doing *everything*. Bug Eyes reported back in such detail that for many years we all—including Alejandro, who never lived up to his dream of growing a beard—considered him our hero.

My parents got worried about what the barrio was doing to their boys. They sold everything down to their socks and bought a proper house in another neighborhood. I lost track of the guys. I never even found out who got to make it with someone from Mary's Bar. I know I didn't.

Living in a decent neighborhood changed everything. At least our parents considered it a decent neighborhood. There wasn't any talking to my new friends about uncouth stuff. Nobody knew what a red-light district was. No one had ever peeked at a girl taking a bath. Not even me.

Meanwhile, deep in my subconscious, the virus of Catholicism spread. Because I had to know everything about sex, my abject ignorance drove me to a Christian bookstore to buy *The Young Man's Book* in the famous Pauline Editions. And there it was that I found my calling. The longer I read the more I understood how much poison I carried in my soul. How many times before had I wanted to be like Estanislao—the only one of us who masturbated—and now I learned how filthy a thing it was.

Every day when classes let out I went to the school yard to keep on learning. I learned that it wasn't good to *flirt*, although it took two weeks more to learn what the word meant. I learned that "nocturnal emissions" were caused by wicked thoughts (it took even more weeks to learn to associate an "emission" with involuntary ejaculation, which was always accompanied by a delightful dream).

I took care not to watch Ramona, our servant, bathing, even though I had already drilled a hole in the bathroom door. Finally, though, I couldn't resist and peeked, only to see nothing at all. Apparently I had miscalculated. So I waited until she emerged, steaming, and went to her room. I immediately grabbed a nail and enlarged the size of the hole, which, the next day, at last let me see what I wanted. Ramona was a round woman, from whichever side you looked at her. Dark, muscular, large-breasted. And she had such a way of washing herself! It almost seemed that she knew someone was watching. She soaped slowly up and down her arms, lingering over her boobs, squeezing the sponge between them till the foam ran down to her . . . well. I stood openmouthed, legs trembling. I watched as she dried herself with chilling slowness. Then I sprinted to my room to struggle with my doubts. This disturbance between my thighs—was there something to do about it?

I told my new friends about my good fortune. Pancho was the first. He stepped right up and enjoyed our little voyeurism (later we learned that Ramona enjoyed it, too). To repay my friendly gesture he invited me to his apartment building to see a neighbor lady naked. When the day came, Pancho arrived all excited. Hurry up! The señora was about to take her bath! I managed to pull on a pair of shorts and rushed to his apartment building.

The door was open. Pancho obviously knew the place

well. He walked in and made himself at home. We sneaked up to the bathroom door, where we heard somebody humming a popular tune. Pancho grabbed me by the arm. Wait just a minute, he whispered, I'm going to ask her. Ask who? The señora, he hissed. I'm the one who hands her the towel. Seriously? She lets you? Of course, he said in exactly the same superior tone I'd heard before from Alejandro. Wait, he said, knocking on the door. Señora, now? She quit humming. She called out with a false note of disgust, Panchito, you *are* a devil. Are you done? he repeated, winking at me. Yes, I'm ready, you ornery little thing. You know where the towel is. Bring it in here and see what happens to you for being a shameless little guy. Pancho cleared his throat and took a deep breath. I can't, Señora. What do you mean you can't? I suppose you want me to come out just like this?

Well, said Pancho, the thing is, I'm here with my best friend, and he's going to hand you the towel. Your friend? she asked, her voice catching. Yes, a friend who wants to meet you. Pancho, you little shit! I told you not to tell anybody. Nicolás is my friend—Pancho explained, as if my name would clear up everything—and he's thirteen. Pancho, you are disgusting. And I'm going to tell your mother. Holy Mary! Sweet Jesus! God, I hope no one finds out! Want me to bring you the towel? Pancho persisted. Help! Somebody's in the bathroom spying on me! Help! Petra, run and tell Doña Sofi! The señora was beside herself. Pancho offered to let me look through the window. But that solved nothing.

The señora ran straight to my friend's house, with her hair still wet. She asked to speak to Doña Sofi, and told her that Pancho had slipped into her bathroom and watched her while she was bathing. Pancho was summoned and given a perfunctory hearing. He explained nothing. While Doña Sofi begged forgiveness for her libertine son, Pancho admitted only to having watched the señora. He was whipped with a belt until he no longer even wanted to go see Ramona. Yet Pancho was absolutely right—how well he knew the female soul!—when he told me that Ramona would wind up asking me to watch her through the peephole. But I had better be very, very careful.

He was correct on both counts. In time the little perforation I had made in the bathroom door turned into a hole that let me view Ramona's dark body just as I wanted to. Now she bathed more often, smiling obscenely and biting her lower lip. Fully aware that I was watching, she bent over and showed off her bottom in absolutely shameless fashion. I never forgave my mother for firing her on the day she found Ramona enlarging the hole even more. Mother supposed Ramona wanted to spy on my father—who in turn had to endure a torrent of mother's abuse—and so I felt bad the day Ramona came to my room to say goodbye.

I'm going, Nicolás. See what your ideas have led to? Yes, I said, and I think it's a bad deal. But didn't we have fun? she winked, taking my hands between hers. I got nervous. Have you received your first Communion? she asked? I thought it a strange question, but coolly nodded that I had. Ramona only gave me the same smile I'd seen when I watched her bathing. She let go of my hands. She pinched my nose and walked away wagging her behind. I never saw her again.

Then Mary showed up. Another dark-skinned, shame-less girl. I fell for her as one can only fall in love at age thir-teen and two months. She paid no attention at all to me. Her boyfriend was a mechanic. When I heard a song by Leo Dan, *Mary Is My Love,* I knew my heart was hers.

Mary was a champion housecleaner. She and I were alone mornings; my brothers were at school, and my par-ents were working. From the dining-room table I watched her bend over to sweep the living-room floor's most hid-den corner, to mop places never mopped before, hiking up her skirt and those undies that hung loose, so very loose. Once after a long session washing dishes, she sat in a stuffed chair. She looked at me for a long time, then asked: How come you study so hard? Because I don't want to be a mechanic, I answered with that spite only the jealous can manage. And those . . . great big books, she smiled, are what you study? Yes. And they're very difficult. And . . . what are you going to be when . . . you're bigger? she asked with her peculiar way of pausing. A doctor. I plan to be a very famous doctor. You shall be Dr. Nicolás Barrientos! she tried to keep on joking. Then she went on. May I address you informally, Dr. Barrientos? Yes. Yes, you may. Do you know where babies come from, Doctor?

The question took me by surprise. Of course I knew where babies came from. I simply didn't know the finer points of the procedure. Studying *The Young Man's Book* had certainly made me a good Christian. It just didn't help with concrete situations. My schoolbooks talked all around the issue. They offered examples of flowers: the male part, the female part, the fertilization by pollen, and all the other processes that produced a lovely flower. But on that one they stood mute.

Of course I know where babies come from, I replied, never lifting my eyes from my Spanish textbook. But . . . do you know how . . . they get made? I started to sweat. This is a barefaced *flirt*, I said to myself. But I wasn't about to confess my ignorance. Sure I know how they get made! Why do you ask? Um . . . well, because I want you to explain it to me, she murmured, mussing my hair. It looks like you know a lot, she gestured at my books. Not at all, I said. I only know that it's a sin. Making babies is a sin? No, doing the, well, the other thing. Haven't you ever done it? Done what? The other thing. What other thing?

You know, she murmured again, squeezing beside me into the narrow chair. Her dress slid much higher than I expected. Her thighs were as dark as those of Ramona, with muscles more defined. Mary, I . . . I began stammering. You're starting to have a beard—she whispered, fingering my still-smooth cheeks—I can feel it. How old are you? Thirteen, going on fourteen. I'll be fourteen in June. In ten months, right? Yes, real soon . . . Mary . . . Mary . . . Mmmmh, she answered in my ear, creating sensations I had never felt. And have you received your first Communion? Yes, but Mary—I felt deliriously naive—we're going to fall. Let's fall then, she said. And we fell.

Once on the floor, she kept on saying things I half understood. As she kept caressing me, I knew for sure that these were the feelings the Pauline Editions condemned with the word *flirt*. But after all, was flirting any worse than swallowing a wafer without having received first Communion? Mary was all over me. She kept saying my name.

Nicolás, Nick, Nicky, she moaned and moaned. My hand wouldn't obey my brain's order to grab at least some part of her. After what seemed like fifteen years, she put her hand right there on my trousers, and I put my hand on her breast. I squeezed lightly, she moaned and squeezed. Lightly. I unbuttoned her blouse. I raised her brassiere and petted her breasts like kitty cats.

Give it to me, she moaned, eyes closed. I looked around, not sure what it was she wanted. Dazed by the warmth and firmness of those fifteen-year-old breasts, I paid no attention. By now her dress was up around her waist. Her underwear was gone. She unbuttoned my pants and yanked them off me. She kept on stroking my . . . well, my parts. Would it offend Christian morals, I wondered, to kiss her breasts? I decided for myself: no. As I kissed them, she kept begging me to give it to her, and I kept wondering what it was she wanted. The way she kept manipulating the region below my belly made me sure I was about to damn myself. But I didn't care. Whatever she wanted to do was fine. When she said something I couldn't quite hear about my "whickerbill," it left me openmouthed. Was it possible that she wanted . . . ? And that's the look I must've had on my face when the door suddenly opened.

But . . . but, what's going on? my mother asked when she saw us on the floor. Quick as a gymnast, Mary stood up and pulled down her wrinkled dress. She tucked those two quivery little kitties back in their bra, coughing as if she'd swallowed a cockroach. Discreetly, with one foot, I pushed the underpants she'd left on the floor under a chair. For a long time afterward I would keep them. Lovingly hidden.

Señora, stammered Mary, I don't know what got into me! Please don't tell my mother. My mother shook her and shouted. Bitch! Child molester! What did you do to my son? Nothing, nothing. We were just playing? Right, Nico? Right, I said, zipping up my pants. We were just playing! Shut up! mother shouted. Go to your room! And I went to my room.

Mary left our house just like Ramona had. Only Mary didn't say good-bye to me. And I remained in love with her. I kept listening to Leo Dan.

Mary kept on seeing her mechanic. And she and I never exchanged another word. A few days later Pancho told me what it meant to have received your first Communion. I told him that, yes, I had done it with Mary, but it was a lie. I hadn't received that sacrament. My mother had prevented it. Anyhow I threw those goddamn underpants of Mary's away four years later, the day I met Alma. Alma was a different type of woman altogether. Immature. She only used me to get things. In exchange for one of the hottest records I've ever heard, the only thing I got out of her were lessons in her specialty: French kissing. Nothing else. Careful with your hands, she said when I tried to get in her bra. It was all very cold. But a promise was a promise. And I gave her my record of Jane Birkin and Serge Gainsbourg: "*Je t'aime, moi non plus*," full of moans that brought back pleasant memories.

They say that life begins at forty. I hope that's true. Before making Life's Biggest Decision, I reread Wolf Wondratschek's forty-three love stories. They fit right into my life:

"Petra jokes around. Barbara shuts up. Andrea is sick of

it all. Isabel is calculating. Eva's always looking around. Nadine talks about it. Edith cries. I have to persuade Catalina beforehand. Tania is afraid. Angela doesn't want to know anything about it. It makes no sense to Carolina, Anke, and Ana. Sabina keeps her hopes up. Ilse controls herself well. Vera can't imagine it. Nina plays hard to get. Alejandra is Alejandra . . ." And so on. For forty-three stories. Except that I never got to number forty-three, Didi, who is always ready.

And that is why—after all my futile efforts—I decided to go down the one path that was waiting for me all along. There was no point in delaying. I was never going to receive that kind of first Communion.

So welcome to the Lord's banquet, my children. Please be seated. In the name of the Father, the Son, and the Holy Spirit, amen. May the Lord be with you. And with your spirit. We are going to examine our consciences. Let us look at our sins.

Translated by Philip Garrison

And One Wednesday

Martha Cerda

ROSA AND AMALIA had anticipated the bells of the seven o'clock mass at the Church of *San Sebastian de Analco* since six o'clock that morning. As they heard the first bell they thanked God that they didn't have to continue tossing and turning in bed. The nights and days seemed endless. They anticipated, with the same anxiety, the mass at seven in the morning as they did the rosary at eight at night, the beginning and end of their daily routine. The thirteen hours in between were dedicated to the prepara-

---

MARTHA CERDA (1945–) was born and lives in Guadalajara. Dramatist, poet, essayist, and novelist, she is also founding director of Guadalajara's Sociedad General de Escritores (Mexico's writers' association) and has served as President of PEN International in Guadalajara. Her books in English are *Señora Rodríguez and Other Worlds* (1997) and *And One Wednesday* (2004), from which this excerpt is taken. Based on the true events of April 22, 1992, when hundreds of Guadalajara's citizens died in an explosion caused by a gas leak, the novel interweaves the stories of ten very different individuals on that single day. It was awarded the Jalisco Prize for Literature.

tion of meals, chores, washing, ironing, and sewing, while hardly speaking to each other.

Rosa will be seventy years old on the first of May, Amalia just turned seventy-one on February fifth, and each was becoming more attached to the house in Analco in which their parents had raised them. Of the old neighbors of that time, some had already passed away and others were now grandparents. Only they had remained unmarried and insisted that the new kids refer to them as *Las señoritas Orozco*. "As though we didn't know the truth about them," they all said, everyone knew the real story despite their superficial sainthood to never give in to the eye of passion. At 6:59 they entered the church, each with a shawl that covered half her face; they took holy water and knelt down one next to the other, looking in opposite directions, anticipating the sound of the last bell.

Rafael had fallen asleep at four o'clock in the morning with his uniform on. At six he woke up yelling, "Did they find him yet?" "Who?" His wife asked. And running to the door, he responded, "The governor." His wife tried to catch up to him with a cup of coffee, but he had already gotten into his truck without saying good-bye. She drank her coffee in the kitchen and was resigned to spend another day alone. The day before, she had hardly spoken with Rafael. When he arrived he told her that he had been looking for the governor in order to report a gas leak in certain streets in Analco such as Gante, Veinte de Noviembre, Aldama and others. In all his years as fire chief, she never saw him so nervous. The good thing was that very soon he would retire and no longer be in harm's way. Although in reality his job was just like any other. As far as she could recall not a single fireman had lost his life since her husband became fire chief. In any case, she would have preferred to marry a shopkeeper who begins work at nine, comes home for lunch in the late afternoon, and returns to work at four and comes back home again at eight o'clock in the evening like everyone else in Guadalajara. But with her husband one never knew. . . .

Rosa and Amalia returned from mass at nine o'clock on Wednesday the twenty-second after taking Communion, praying to San Francisco, and purchasing their provisions as usual in the local market, one piece of pumpkin pie and one sweet potato covered with honey. Arriving home, they fought, as usual, over who gets the squash and who gets the sweet potato. "Why didn't you tell me, I could have gotten you one," they repeated to each other almost every day. Today was Rosa's turn to make lunch, and as always, she would make *tortas* with squash and minced vegetables, which Amalia detested. Then they would knit until it was time again to say the rosary. When they came back from church they would cover the canary cages and rinse off the patio. In order to organize their bills before they went to bed they would have to hurry up with their dinner, which normally consisted of sweet bread and coffee with cream. Rosa could already taste the sweet bread that she ordered from the bakery and could not wait to dip it into her coffee.

In general they didn't watch television, but that Wednesday Amalia was more willing to annoy her sister for some reason. Seventy years of putting up with her and accommodating her every inclination had resulted in a deep hatred for her sister, but at the same time she couldn't live without her. The best way to annoy her was to sit in front of her while she was cooking. At nine thirty Amalia turned on the television, knowing very well that Rosa would do everything in her power to make as much noise as possible while she was cooking to annoy her. That's why Amalia turned the volume up as high as it would go and didn't hear Rosa when she said, "I feel dizzy from that gasoline smell," or when she fainted and fell on the ground and then said nothing.

Rafael reproached himself for having overslept. Tuesday night he investigated, along with his men, a wide area between the streets of Gante and Veinte de Noviembre all the way to the Atlas neighborhood, looking for a gas leak which they never found. There was no time to lose, the neighbors had been complaining about the smell of gasoline for the past three days. Just down the street they came upon a Pemex plant and some factories. There they encountered reporters from two newspapers, *El Informador* and *Siglo XXI*. The Pemex experts stated that everything was under control, and Rafael was suddenly enraged. He didn't know what was going on exactly, but if he were governor he would have had the entire area evacuated. Unfortunately, he wasn't and even after he left his house he still had not heard from the governor, or the mayor for that matter. Who was going to handle this problem? Rafael walked directly into the area at risk as many families started getting up. He arrived at seven o'clock and immediately started his calculations: explosive danger, one hundred percent. Opening the sewer vents hadn't worked; he would then flood the pipes with water to neutralize the gasoline, but where would it go? The natural incline of the pipes would take the mixture directly into the downtown area. "Where the hell were those Pemex bastards? They already knew what was going on and they could help solve the problem!"

With each question, time was running out and the clock struck nine. The milk vendors, butchers, bakers, grocery stores, mechanics, food courts, pharmacies, and hair salons all opened their doors. The people walked right by Rafael and said hello to him. His presence there reassured them. Guadalajara, Mexico's second largest city, was a safe place to live. . . .

Despite the volume Amalia fell asleep in front of the television. When she finally woke up she didn't hear any noise in the kitchen. "That Rosa," she thought, "must have gone out to the patio to eat something else. She is so immature. Her nephews take advantage of this naïveté to encourage her to buy another house. They have no idea how much this one is worth. In every wall there is more gold than one could count. But they're going to have to earn it. Lazy bastards, while I am still alive they are not going to get a dime," Amalia said in a loud voice so that Rosa would hear her. Amalia waited another minute as she counted in her head what her debtors owed her. "Three million pesos. I would rather flog myself than give that money to those assholes," Amalia said—as she got up from her armchair and went toward the kitchen to surprise Rosa.

When they were kids they used to play hide and seek

and Rosa always won. She always won those spring pageants as well. Friends of the family always said how she was the cute little blonde with blue eyes. As for Amalia, on the other hand, she was the smart one. She would never get chosen to play the part of the Virgin Mary or the flower girl at weddings like her sister. For this reason she became her father's right hand even before she was twenty years old. And when he died Amalia took his place. "If we had just had a boy . . ." her mother used to say. And Amalia always beat herself up for having been born too weak to be a man and too ugly to be a woman. The latter could not be remedied but the former had possibilities. For example, she manipulated her sister and made her call off her engagement two days before the wedding. All to show that beauty was no match for power. She made Rosa promise that she would not lose her innocence and never become the victim of secrets as she had. In order to avoid any possibility of a future love, Amalia let Rosa get a cat that became the talk and scandal of the family when it suddenly had kittens. Rosa never said a word but she was never the same after Amalia killed all of the kittens and had the cat spayed. This was the same cat that jumped on Amalia as she entered the kitchen and saw Rosa lying on the floor, this day, Wednesday, the twenty-second of April, 1992, at ten o'clock in the morning. One minute before an explosion killed Amalia.

Rafael felt as though his head were about to explode as he heard the screams, the glass breaking, and the pipes bursting open. Then he felt the ground sinking in under him as his mind became silent. What was happening to the houses, the automobiles, and the people who were stand-

ing over there just a second ago? Rafael tried to run away
but he kept falling and getting back up again. Men,
women, and children ran alongside him, all frantically pan-
icking. I must be going crazy, Rafael thought, not allowing
the falling stones, cement, warped pieces of metal, or people in pain stop him in any way. Where am I? Rafael asked
himself as he tried to get somewhere safe. There was nothing, no sidewalks, no streets and no stoplights. The next
explosion left Rafael on his back and knocked the wind out
of him as he searched in the depths of his throat for his
deepest cry: "God help us!" Little by little tears started
down his face, sobs and finally words: "Get out of here, as
far as possible," a deafened Rafael cried out. He looked
around for his firemen but he didn't see them anywhere.
All he saw was a child with his mouth open trying to
scream in vain. Rafael picked him up in his arms and kept
on running. How far did the explosion hit? Would his wife
and children still be alive? Then he suddenly heard someone say "Boss," but Rafael didn't associate it with himself
until it was repeated many times and a couple of men put
him in a patrol car. The first thing he asked was, "Did they
find the governor yet?" . . .

The ten foot walls, concealing what was happening inside
the apartment, fell on Amalia who was unable to reach
Rosa and yell to her: "Get up, don't play games." Amalia
no longer thought of her childhood, her nephews, her
debtors, and there she died, reflecting the image of Rosa's
cat in her pupils. The smell of gasoline penetrated the air
but it no longer mattered. Just like none of the resentment
mattered anymore or the squash *tortas*, the blue eyes or the

seven o'clock mass. The only important thing now was Rosa, who then came to but could not see a thing in front of her. I must be under the table, she said to herself as she recognized the wooden legs. It was the same table she used to hide under as a child. She couldn't understand how the years had gone by, but she wasn't frightened because she heard her cat meowing. "Minina, Minina," she called out to her. The cat was exactly eight feet on top of her. Rosa counted to ten as she used to do when she and Amalia used to play hide and seek. She won't find me, Rosa was sure, remembering the few times she heard the words: "I got you," from Amalia's lips. If she wanted to get away from her, she always offered to play hide and seek. That's why she was surprised by the voices that said: "Look over there where the cat is digging, there must be someone there." Rosa just waited without making any noise. "Maybe they'll leave and I'll win again," she thought. When they removed the debris and got her out of there, the cat started to purr. A man then asked Rosa if there was anyone else in the house, so they could continue the search. Rosa answered, "No, I lived alone." And she took off with her cat in her arms.

Translated by Carl I. Jubrán

It Is Nothing of Mine

Araceli Ardón

TERESITA DEL NIÑO JESÚS RODRÍGUEZ made this sentence immortal for she said it in front of the whole world on the most important day of her life.

As a girl, Tere had been marked by the death of her older brother. They were young and she barely understood what had happened. But she suffered from her father's grief, for he had the misfortune to live yearning for this son who would have been his heir, successor, and companion. Certainly, he would have been a superb horseman, masterfully wielding the lasso to perform the most audacious stunts: not only would he have roped cattle; he would have been cold-blooded enough to execute "the pass of death,"

ARACELI ARDÓN (1958–) was born in San Miguel de Allende. She is the author of the novel *Historias íntimas de la casa de Don Eulogio* (1998); a biography, *Semblanza: Roberto Ruiz Obregón* (2001); and a children's book, *La pandilla de Miguel* (2002). For her work in the cultural magazine *Ventana de Queré-taro* she was awarded the Rosario Castellanos National Prize for Journalism and Literature in 1988. She lives in Querétaro, where she has been a professor of Spanish since 1980.

---

that is, to ride out of the corral bareback alongside a bronco and, coming up close to it, leap from one to the other, hanging on only by their manes.

Manuel Rodríguez had been destined to inherit the best ranch in the region, with hundreds of Holsteins, quarter horses, enormous hogs—which were slaughtered on the premises—and a flock of sheep fed and cared for on a whim: to make the smoothest and most delicious cheese to spread on the Sunday hors d'oeuvres.

But Manuel died in early childhood, attacked by fevers his small body could not fend off. Teresita, his sister and five years his junior, became the erroneous heir—erroneous because she could never be the agile and authoritative horseman her father needed to preserve his lineage.

Nevertheless, little by little, time cured Señor Rodríguez of his grief, and his daughter's laughter had the desired effect: it was a balm for his wounds, a tiny tinkling bell that rang all through the house. At unexpected moments, there was the music of her piano, and she was the first of a bouquet of her friends, darling girls who came to spend their vacations at the ranch, when Tere was let out of her convent school.

When Tere finished junior high school, her parents decided to buy a house in Querétaro, right on the Avenida de Independencia. Her mother, Doña Laura, could attend mass at San Francisco Church, pray at La Congregación, and practice her Spiritual Exercises in the convent of Santa Cruz de los Milagros; furthermore—of course—here the girl could study, make quality friendships, get married, and perhaps soon, with God's help, have many children. Then, with her large family, she would return to the ranch to live in the big house and oversee the planting, the peach harvest, and the care of the livestock.

"Your daughter is a gem," the very proud mother would say to her husband, knowing that there was something of a trade-off.

"She has made me happy," the father would say. "For an old man, there is no better love than that of the women in his house."

Tere learned so much in so few years that others could not help but notice: she became an expert at embroidery; she could play Chopin as if Polish blood ran in her veins; and she spoke French with Monsieur Aubert, a descendant of Maximilian's photographer and the founding teacher of Querétaro's Alliance Française. Tere knew that she was at a disadvantage in life. She lived with the oil portrait of her dead brother presiding over the dining room. And what's more, between her soft, honeyed eyes and the curve of her beautiful lips, right next to her nose, Tere had a wart that would have ruined the life of any other girl.

In those days, there was no plastic surgery. And men, as if *they* were perfect, were exacting and domineering with their girlfriends. Never mind how they were with their wives.

So Tere had to content herself with being doubly studious, diligent, pleasant, and merry. She had to accept her role as bridesmaid when her closest friends married. And when Juvenal Monraz stepped into her life, she gave thanks to San Antonio the matchmaker, and to Santa Rita de Casia, the Augustinian nun who grants the impossible. Santa Rita was in fashion; she had been canonized in May of 1900 and now, thirty years later, she did not yet have so many prayers in Heaven and thus she had time to perform the most spectacular miracles.

"Juvenal is a miracle," said Chole and Maru, Teresita's best friends.

"I'd like one like him for my aunt, Yola," lamented Chole, sincerely grieved by the misfortune of her good, home-loving, and hardworking aunt.

"He's handsome, Tere. I like his square chin, well-cut ears, almost aquiline nose; a very Arabic look," said Maru, whose husband was of Turkish descent and had a penetrating gaze.

According to the "old boys" who met in the café in front of the main square, her suitor was nothing more than a loafer in search of a meal ticket for life. They knew Juvenal well: he was one of them.

For the suitor, it was relatively easy to conquer Señorita Rodríguez. In full view of the town, he strolled with her on his arm, serenaded her once a month, sent her white roses, then yellow roses, and finally, for her birthday, he sent her red roses. He bought her corsages of gardenias to adorn her hand on summer afternoons. In short, he fulfilled each and every one of the rituals of courtship with elegance and precision.

Tere knew that two square centimeters of misshapen flesh condemned her to rushing to accept this chance to marry, for it was a chance that would not come again. And for many years, she did not regret it.

For Juvenal was a good husband. He was considerate enough to allow her to have her own room, visit her friends and attend their get-togethers every month, and buy an automobile and drive it three times a week to the ranch, while he sat on the passenger side because she enjoyed driving and he did not want the responsibility of risking an accident that might scratch its brilliant finish.

When her father died, Tere suggested to her husband that they move to her parents' house to keep her mother company. Juvenal agreed with pleasure and this convinced Tere, as she told her closest friends, that she had truly won the lottery. By this time, the others had to put up with contempt, rudeness, brooding silences, infidelities (even with the maids), and sometimes beatings. Some had been abandoned for a while and, after their husbands had finished with their adventures, had had to take them back, though the women hid this with discretion and lies. And what's more, Juvenal had even forgiven Tere for being barren. Despite all their attempts—at siesta time, at night, even at dawn, in traditional positions and in others out of a circus—she could not get pregnant. Señora Monraz continued to endure the emptiness inside her. Nothing could allay her grief, not even her husband's goodness that had allowed her to keep her ranch, her house, and her car.

The doctors diagnosed an immature womb and suggested treatments that she followed to the letter. Finally, sadly, she had to accept it. She had no little ones to care for, no birthday piñatas to make, no first Communion parties to attend, and so, no choice but to accompany her mother to say the rosary.

Yes, Juvenal generously forgave her for all of it. The only thing this good husband asked for was the free use of his own time. After breakfast, while she met with the old ranch manager in the office, he read the newspaper. Then, while they walked together to the Jardín Obregón (which was at that time the main plaza, flanked by three bank buildings), he would comment on the day's important news. Her briefcase in hand, she would leave to make the deposits and necessary transfers, always confident that her husband, the respected man all women should have by their side, was waiting for her nearby, or at a distance of no more than one hundred meters, having his shoes shined.

After lunch he would have his siesta, and in the afternoons he would go out to play cards and dominoes. As did all the men.

Other husbands invited him to their houses for poker weekends. Sometimes the women joined them, trying their luck with Uruguayan canasta. There were couples who knew how to play the best hands, always defeating their opponents and raking in the chips. In that city of seventy thousand pious souls, one had to relieve the tedium with something.

Juvenal was so prudent and discreet, he had such respect for his wife and his home, that it never occurred to him to invite his buddies, for they might behave badly, disturb his invalid mother-in-law, or tell off-color jokes that might be heard by Teresita's delicate ears.

So he met his gambling friends in different places until eight at night, when his wife received him at home and served him his supper. They would then spend a pleasant evening, sometimes in the company of family friends, until they went to sleep peacefully.

Furthermore, as Tere would tell her friends—all of them envious of her good husband— Juvenal was an ocean of generosity: a good part of their produce went to some orphans.

"Do you know them?" one asked maliciously.

"Don't even bring it up. Juvenal doesn't like to talk about it. He says your left hand should not know what your right hand is doing."

And so it was that the Monraz's buoyant finances sprang a little leak: cheeses for the orphans, fruits for the orphans. And, of course, there was also the money Juvenal lost at gambling. This man had no luck at cards. But he would docilely come home to his wife—his mind exhausted from so many calculations, Teresita thought, as she obliged him with a generous glass of sherry to begin the evening.

"Unlucky at cards . . . ," her husband would say, giving her the chance to finish the adage.

Twenty years went by. Teresita buried her mother in the Rodríguez family tomb, and at forty years old she began to ask herself what she could fill her days with besides hats, coats, and gloves, which were seldom worn in Querétaro. There were so few occasions: elegant weddings, bullfights with matadors of international fame, dances with full orchestras.

Then Santa Rita (who before becoming a nun was a widow) took Juvenal away with her. This husband of fifty-some years had a considerably expanded waistline, for he scarcely walked even the few blocks between his most pressing appointments. He had done no exercise, not even in the countryside, having given up riding at the same time as he had taken up the habit of smoking cigars.

And it was of an aggressive cancer in the center of his right lung that, one Saturday at midday, Juvenal died.

Teresita cried oceans. She called together her notary, her confessor, her manager, and the expert cook who had prepared her banquets. She arranged to have the casket taken to the new funeral home on the Calle Hidalgo. It was the latest fashion in a town used to mourning their dead at home. On some matters, Teresita was in the vanguard. She made an arrangement with the sacristan of La Merced, ordered a lavish display of white flowers, and brought in the chef of the Grand Hotel to take care of the friends who came to offer their condolences.

That night, wearing a black suit—meant for a trip to the capital for a concert in Bellas Artes—and a black high-collared lace blouse, which made her skin appear even whiter, Tere told anecdotes of her life with her husband over and over again. She emphasized his kindness, his acts of generosity.

The next morning she received her mother-in-law, her brothers- and sisters-in-law, and Juvenal's nephews and nieces, the only children who had enjoyed the new swimming pool at the ranch. She was a most gracious hostess to all, the most upright widow, with a strength shown only by the most spiritually advanced.

Then, at one o'clock in the afternoon, a woman in mourning arrived sobbing and shuddering, followed by two boys and a girl, all of whom had square chins, well-cut ears, almost aquiline noses—in short, a very Arabic look. The children drew close. The boys were wearing well-cut suits made of wool and cashmere; the little girl was in a dress with white ruffles. They did not need to say anything. In the expectant silence, the crowd of neighbors and friends parted to let them pass. They all watched as the woman and her children took their places at the four corners of the coffin, each beside a flickering candle.

Teresita, once having recovered from the confusion and with all her questions answered, rose from her seat, took five steps to where Juvenal lay in his box, and said in a loud voice: "It is nothing of mine." She went out into the sunny street followed by her faithful manager, leaving the dead husband in the hands of his secret family.

All of Querétaro could draw its own conclusions about the case that was, for more than a year, juicier than anything on the radio soap operas. They knew all the details, both real and made-up, about the doings of Juvenal Monraz. His widow, meanwhile, had a long stay in Paris, where at last she practiced the French she had learned from Monsieur Aubert.

Translated by C. M. Mayo

Fata Morgana

Bruno Estañol

I TURNED ELEVEN years old on the first of January 1956.

In those days, three elements tended to influence the children around here: our river, popular music, and the movies.

Foremost among these was the river: a great river, wide, murky, and mighty; a river one kilometer wide; a river with an island in the middle, Isla del Buey; a river that spills out into the ocean after traveling fourteen kilometers; a river full of living creatures; a river in which one can fish, swim, and sail; a river that splits up into hundreds of tributaries;

BRUNO ESTAÑOL (1945–) was born in Frontera, Tabasco, and educated in medicine and neuroscience at Mexico City's National Autonomous University and at Johns Hopkins Medical School in Baltimore, Maryland. His literary career began in 1989 with the publication of *Fata Morgana*, a novel—from which this excerpt is taken—set in his hometown in 1956. He has published several works of fiction since then, including *Ni el reino de otro mundo* (1991), *El féretro de cristal* (1992), *La esposa de Martín Butchell* (1997), *La barca de oro* (1998), and *Passiflora Incarnata* (2003). He lives in Mexico City.

a river that has been navigated since time immemorial. The Maya used to travel up the Usumacinta and the Grijalva and the Mexican Gulf Coast in their canoes. Ours is an excellent river for navigation, like the Nile or the Mississippi. Huge paddlewheel steamboats used to plow up and down the river in the days of my youth. When the sun rises on our river, residents of the riverbank can be seen paddling their numerous canoes. Ours is a treacherous river in which many children have drowned, a river full of fish: *bobos*, *banderudos*, *lovinas*, *topotas*, sea bream, and horse mackerel. Those who live near our river will inevitably have to confront it. At some point they must learn to swim. At some point they will learn to fish. At some point they will sail to San Juan Bautista, Veracruz, Puerto México, Progreso, Campeche, Tampico, Brownsville, or New Orleans. Swimming across our river is considered a great feat. Children who accomplish this become local heroes. Being a good swimmer is both prestigious and practical. Fishing is an activity that is also practiced in this port. There exists an uncatchable fish. In the depths of the river, under the pier, lies the great stone bass. Huge and heavy, it devours everything that crosses its path, but it will never be hooked. Fishing is an incessant activity here. We fish with a variety of tackle: hooks, fishnets, dragnets, creel, baskets, lures, bait, and spears. Ours is an historic river. The Maya, the Phoenicians of the Americas, conducted their commercial activities here. Hernán Cortés sailed down this river, and here he founded Santa María de la Victoria and received La Malinche. Boats loaded with tropical timber—cedar, mahogany, primrose, and guaiacum—arrive and depart via this river. Our great river has been the principal avenue of transportation and communication in this area for centuries. Fata Morgana arrived by way of this river. The mention of her name still causes me to tremble. Fata Morgana! An aura of mystery surrounds her. She is beautiful. She is a great dancer. She had been a Nazi spy. Who knows what she is doing now in these lands infested with mosquitoes and parasites? Fata Morgana is German and blonde and came here from Veracruz. No one knows why she emigrated from Europe to our continent. What could she possibly have been spying on in these lowlands crawling with lizards, iguanas, and caimans? Around here the verb "to spy" means to peer out furtively from behind windows and doors, to see without being seen. All the windows around here have shutters and the front doors have peepholes. When a man is walking down the street there are sure to be many eyes upon him. In this town everything is discovered thanks to the act of spying. What would a German spy have been doing here? Nobody knows. It's a secret. After all, one spies in order to know what other people do not know.

Fata Morgana: a mirage that draws sailors to their doom. Fata Morgana: a cruel mirage, richly decorated like all mirages. Fata Morgana: the future, our inevitable rendezvous with death. Morgana: the fairy or sprite of Irish mythology. Morgan la Fey of the Arthurian cycle, symbol of the femme fatale. According to my brother Pedro Ángel, the name is indicative of an ominous herald, such as Marlene Dietrich in *The Blue Angel*; or the legendary mirage in the Strait of Messina, where people, houses, and boats have been known to suddenly appear upon the water, sometimes flying, sometimes suspended, sometimes slowly drifting across the sky; or the Xtabay of the Maya, *vagina dentata*, mirage, mirror, golden epiphany, divine incarnation, the unattainable, eternal temptation.

Fata Morgana! Ladies and gentlemen. A marvelous spectacle. A surreal, fascinating woman. Come and see her tonight at the grand Union Theater!

"What's a quick-change artist?"

"Don't you know? It's a dancer who changes clothes quickly behind a folding screen and comes out dressed to match the music. If the music is Russian she dresses like a Russian, and if it's Spanish she dresses perhaps as a Galician, and she can change her appearance nearly instantaneously." Pedro Ángel explained this to me with a toothpick in his mouth and a sardonic smile. He had just turned eighteen and had graduated from high school, so he thought that he knew it all.

"I thought that changing was when one thing becomes another."

"No, silly, that's what the alchemists used to believe. It's really simply an appearance of change. You have to know about logic and epistemology."

"Logic and what?"

"Listen, Fata Morgana is a mirage that appears in the Mediterranean and lures sailors to their death. This lady is a hallucination, a mirage, hers is merely an act of prestidigitation using elegant costumes. Fata Morgana isn't German or anything of the sort, believe me, she's probably a striptease dancer from Tivoli or a lousy whore from Biscay."

"Guess who's playing the music at her show?"

"A band?"

"Nope, Fata Morgana wanted only a pianist."

"In that case, it's going to be María Pía."

"That's right. I'm going to the Union tonight because it's my birthday, and I'll be turning the pages for her."

The Union Theater could have appeared in a Hollywood Western. It was made entirely of wood, who knows how long ago? There was a large window in the rear and some box seats to the sides. It also had a mezzanine, which was cheaper and had a separate entrance. It was a miracle that the gypsy moths and termites had not devoured the place long ago, given its exclusively wooden construction. The children enjoyed stomping rhythmically on the wood floor during the Sunday matinees, when they used to show Flash Gordon in *The Invasion of Mongo* or *The Underwater Empire*, or when the hero was riding off to rescue the heroine at full gallop in the Westerns. Children only had two choices in those days: the radio or the cinema. I always chose the latter. Ever since turning eight I would go to the movies daily, except Fridays and Sundays because the place used to fill up on weekends. All the great Mexican and American films played there. I grew up surrounded by phantasmagoria, the chimerical stories of the silver screen. But now this great theater was going to be used for a dance performance. The quick-change artist Fata Morgana was going to appear in person. Everyone wanted to see her. Women rushed to the beauty parlors to have their hair done. Men took out their naphthalene-scented suits and ties from the closet. Since it was raining that night, everyone carried umbrellas or parasols, and wore raincoats, and the floor of the theater became extremely slippery, like an ice rink, due to the quantity of mud trailing behind the spectators' boots and shoes. Some of the gentlemen in the audience were glancing up nervously at the mezzanine, fearing perhaps that one of the "plebes" might try to urinate on them. More tickets than the number of seats available were sold, and those in the mezzanine began to shout anxiously:

"Come on! Let's get this show started!"

The piano stood to the right of the stage. My aunt, María Pía, arranged her sheet music. The first piece: "Slow Waltz" by Leo Delibes. The second: "Fire Dance" by Manuel de Falla. The third: "Oh Chichornia," the Russian folksong. The fourth: "Hungarian Dance no. 5" by Liszt. Then: "Song of India" by Rimsky-Korsakov, and later there were others that I can no longer remember. The restless ones in the mezzanine began stomping their feet, causing dust to descend over the more genteel spectators. A flurry of insults was exchanged between the two groups. The orchestra began to play a reveille, the same one that was played at all civic ceremonies and at the close of each school year. Then the radiant Fata Morgana appeared. She was not in the least disappointing. She wore the tutu of a classical ballerina. Her blond hair was pulled back and gathered at the nape of her neck. She danced as if she were a doll or a puppet, performing pirouettes and *jetés*. When the first piece was over she hurried behind a folding screen that had been placed provisionally on the stage. The orchestra started to play a reveille again, and before it was over the magnificent Fata Morgana came out in Spanish costume, or, more specifically, in traditional Castilian garb. A mantilla and ornamental comb crowned her blond head. Her bobbing head and stomping feet perfectly interpreted a composition by Manuel de Falla. After that, the band played another reveille: *Miss ladybug married a dandy rooster and their children came out with a coat and a cane, singing "la-dee-da, in the morning, la-dee-da-dee-da."*

Immediately thereafter, Fata Morgana came out dressed as a Russian peasant, and the first notes of "Oh Chichornia" sounded, slow and melancholic. Later, the dynamic of the music rose to a crescendo, and the tempo reached a frenetic pace. She would look better in a veil, I thought, remembering how it had been performed in the movies. Suddenly, Fata Morgana stopped dancing. She knelt down on the stage and began searching frantically for something, while the music continued and the folks in the gallery started shouting and whistling. Then the music stopped and the master of ceremonies came out.

"Due to forces beyond our control the function must be temporarily suspended."

The audience responded by pelting him with an avalanche of sucked oranges and guava. It was announced over a megaphone that the function would be permanently canceled due to the incivility of the audience. Rumors spread that some kind of paraphernalia related to espionage had dropped from her clothes, a piece of microfilm or something like that. Maybe she simply lost one of her earrings or suffered a sudden attack of colic. Who knows.

Translated by Eduardo Jiménez

Twins

Ilan Stavans

AT DAWN OF THAT DAY in August when Los Caprichos restaurant burned down, Diego Cherem was locked up in a prison in the city of Acutzingo and the cadaver of his twin brother, Gamal, was in the morgue.

The restaurant had been the focus of an act of revenge. Its reputation was widely known outside the republic and upon stepping outside, one would undoubtedly see tour buses parked outside the door. The *tamales de elote, mole poblano, sopa de frijol,* and the *pescado a la veracruzana* on the menu were incomparable. These dishes were yielding

ILAN STAVANS (1961–), a descendant of Eastern European Jews, was born in Mexico City. He is the Lewis-Sebring Professor of Latin American and Latino Culture at Amherst College. He books include *The Hispanic Condition* (1995), *On Borrowed Words* (2001), *Spanglish* (2003), and *Dictionary Days* (2005). He has edited numerous anthologies including *Tropical Synogogues: Short Stories by Jewish Latin American Writers* (1994) and *The Poetry of Pablo Neruda* (2003). His short fiction is collected in *The One-Handed Pianist and Other Stories* (1996). *The Essential Ilan Stavans* was published in 2000.

an enormous fortune for the owner, a bald Lebanese immi-
grant who had been a soccer player before opening, with
borrowed money, the taco stand of the same name where
Los Caprichos would later flourish.

His wife had died giving birth to the twins and it was he
who had raised them. Since they were young, Gamal and
Diego had helped in the kitchen of the restaurant, washed
dishes in the courtyard sink, or tended the register. They
were handsome, had aquiline noses, chestnut-colored hair,
and were obese, like their father, who while the consommé
was being prepared in the stewpot or the tortillas were being
toasted in the flat clay pan, tasted large mouthfuls and
advised when there was too much salt or not enough lemon,
if the chicken was too spicy or the guacamole needed more
onion. To eat well and abundantly was his principal need.

One of his sources of pride though, perhaps the major
one, was the very intimate fraternal bond between his sons.
When one of them was given a bicycle as a gift, he shared
it with the other in exchange for a couple of hours with the
electric train. They would go to the barber shop together
and dressed the same. Their bond also manifested itself in
an emotional manner: if Gamal traveled to Tuxtla by himself to visit their maternal grandparents, Diego would
become depressed and have trouble eating; if one of them
had an accident, no matter how minor, the other one predicted it from miles away and seconds in advance. It was
difficult to tell the difference between them and people
confused their names. Nevertheless, their father knew who
was who: Diego had a scar on his right pinkie that the doctor had discovered moments after his birth, was quarrel-
some, liked biology and maps, and was very moody;

Gamal, in turn, was more charismatic and preferred sports to education, even though he was good at arithmetic and added quickly. For example, during a dispute over a Swiss aluminum jackknife that was kept in a drawer in their father's dresser and that had been a gift from a patron, Diego's vindictive disposition caused him to appropriate it, arguing that he would use it for personal protection. Meanwhile, Gamal resigned himself to a soccer ball, assuring that if he was attacked he would defend himself with his bare fists, without weapons.

When they were seventeen their close bond was broken into a thousand pieces by the appearance of a woman. It was during a school party. Diego was ill and didn't attend. A friend of Gamal's who had a cousin recently arrived from Guadalajara called him over to a corner and introduced them. Unembarrassed, Gamal asked her to dance; they talked and fell in love. In an effort not to make Diego jealous, Gamal kept his courtship a secret, always thinking up another excuse whenever he went out with her to the movies or took her to eat ice cream. Diego, as expected, intuited the mystery but kept his jealousy to himself. Weeks later, while the couple was walking by a large self-service department store, the girl stopped to go to the bathroom. It was a pure coincidence (or perhaps it was intentional, it's impossible to know) that five minutes later, Gamal watched how his girlfriend ran to his brother, who had suddenly appeared in front of a tie counter, hugged him, and practically kissed him. It was simply a case of mistaken identity, but the poor woman was so surprised that she started to cry hysterically. Diego apologized and excused himself, quickly disappearing into the crowd.

A month later Gamal's girlfriend indirectly provoked an altercation. It began with a discussion about which of the two brothers would open the restaurant for two weeks because their father had to travel to Houston for some medical tests. Neither of them wanted to do it (you had to wake up early) and the heated discussion that had started in a bedroom ended in a fist fight in the living room. Gamal, who had a bruised eye and was furious, went up to the second floor, opened his brother's armoire, took the money he had saved in a money box, rushed out slamming the door, and spent it. Diego swore he would get revenge. He followed through the next afternoon by unexpectedly appearing at Gamal's girlfriend's side pretending to be Gamal and then taking advantage of her. Given this unfortunate scenario it's easy to envision an atmosphere of animosity with horrible consequences.

Their father did what he could to resolve the situation, but he wasn't successful. Gamal moved to a hotel, enrolled in the university, which he didn't attend for very long, dedicated himself to helping in the management of Los Caprichos, and became addicted to billiards and betting on horses. His love affairs multiplied and became volatile at the same time. Diego sold his possessions and traveled to Africa, Asia, and South America. Every three months his letters arrived from Buenos Aires, Marrakech, or Egypt, or he would call from Medellín or Damascus. Those people who had seen Gamal in person and a photograph of Diego were sure that both of them had gained weight excessively; their faces were increasingly ugly and now it was easy to physically recognize the difference between them.

They didn't see each other for years, perhaps a decade.

Their father died. Relatives and friends traveled to the city to attend the funeral. The event was replete with tears and consternation when the family discovered that the heart attack brought on by obesity that befell the restaurateur and cut his life short at age fifty-one, also left him without a will. With a belly that caused him to pop the buttons off his shirt, Diego returned from Alaska and ignored his brother for the seven days the mourning lasted. They merely exchanged insults when Diego brought a real estate agent to appraise their late father's mansion and Gamal refused to open the door to them.

The relatives dried their tears and then they dispersed. The suitable approach would have been for the twins to divide the money and property. But they didn't do it. Gamal decided that because he had managed Los Caprichos for years, he should be the one to inherit the business. He was willing to give his brother an annuity in an effort to keep him quiet and out of sight.

The situation was not going to be so simple. There was too much stored-up rancor.

On the afternoon that Gamal arrived at the restaurant and started to give orders, the employees obeyed him until Diego arrived shouting:

"I challenge you here and now. A contest will decide who will be the future owner of the restaurant. Choose the kind of battle you want to engage in." He was wearing a black raincoat with a cameo pinned on the lapel and a beret that covered his premature baldness.

His visit was so brief that he didn't even give his brother time to respond. The next day he received a sealed envelope:

they would have dinner together alone in the restaurant. They would eat until they were full, until they were dead.

Despite the fact that the challenge sounded stupid, the twins carried it out to its end. The date and time they agreed upon was August 11 at two o'clock. It was raining outside. Gamal Cherem, who at age thirty-four weighed 289 pounds, arrived three minutes early. He was carrying a soaking wet umbrella and gabardine, which he handed to the waiter, and greeted the others. Then, he went over to the table that he had selected for the site of the contest. He had selected it the night before for its proximity to fresh air from a window and because it was a step away from the restroom. He thought about which would be the most suitable chair and sat down, nervous. Diego arrived afterward, wearing the same raincoat, cameo, and beret he had worn during his last visit, and sat down on the remaining chair without looking at his opponent.

One of them snapped his fingers and a waiter brought the menu. For an aperitif, there was *sangría*, *agua de orchata*, *bolillos con mantequilla*, *tacos de carnitas*, and *jícamas con limón*. The appetizer: *sopa de camarones*, *sopa de frijoles*, and *tamales de elote*. The main course: *pollo en mole poblano*, *quesadillas*, *enchiladas verdes*, *ensalada de nopales*, *chiles rellenos de cochinita pibil*, *pescado a la veracruzana*, *tacos de cabrito con guacamole*, *gorditas pellizcadas con manteca* and *chiles en nogada*. For dessert: *flan* and *arroz con leche* and *merengue*. The food had been placed near the table in a glass case under a low flame, which kept it hot.

The brothers agreed on the food selection and then Gamal sent the waiters away. The last waiter to leave closed the door and only the silence between the rivals remained in the restaurant. The contest began. Meanwhile, it had stopped raining outside.

The glass case was opened and they each took their ration without exchanging a word. It was a rule that they had to eat the same amount of food in whatever time they wanted without leaving a single bread crumb on the table-cloth.

The clock hands showed four o'clock, seven, eight. The twins weren't even up to dessert. Neither of them was giving up, even though their paleness and decreased appetites were obvious. From time to time, Diego placed his hand in his pocket and felt an object. The tension was high. A bit of humanity would have resolved it, but the brothers were determined to kill each other by mouthfuls.

It was while chewing fish, lukewarm after sitting on the table for so long, that Diego pretended to have a bone lodged in his throat and stood up. Gamal raised his arms in a triumphant gesture. His jubilation didn't last long. With controlled momentum, Diego thrust a Swiss jack-knife into Gamal's chest and killed him. Crazed, he nevertheless went to the kitchen and lit fire with a matchstick to a pile of napkins and then did the same to the curtains and cupboard. He dragged his brother's cadaver to the courtyard, and, while he was laughing, allowed himself to be hypnotized by the flames that were ascending toward the ceilings and walls. This sad spectacle revealed itself to the residents of Acutzingo in the form of fluttering ashes in the night air.

The next day appeared damp and quiet.

Translated by Harry Morales

Tarantula

Raymundo Hernández-Gil

THROUGHOUT THE VILLAGE, an unusual feeling of peace filled the air. Many years had passed since the villagers had felt such peace. They were celebrating the death of the village witch. By all accounts, and to be perfectly frank, they had all yearned for her death. They had not been able to live worry-free knowing that she was interfering with people's lives. Almost no one attended the wake, except those who felt compelled either by curiosity or morbid satisfaction. The house where the body was dis-

RAYMUNDO HERNÁNDEZ-GIL (1965–) was born in Sayula de Alemán, Veracruz, where the majority used to speak Popoluca as its first language. When he was thirteen, he and his family moved to the city of Minatitlán. In 1994, after returning to Mexico from the United States, he was able to begin studies at the University of Veracruz (Minatitlán) medical school; however, he withdrew and returned to the United States, determined that neither poverty nor the difficulties of language and culture would hold him back. In 2002, at the age of thirty-eight, he graduated with a bachelor's degree in Spanish translation and Latin American literature. Today he works in Utah as a medical translator. His work has been published in the Brigham Young University student journal, *La Marca Hispánica*.

played had a strange cast, not at all inviting. The walls seemed to encase an alien feeling. The house was made of mud bricks, with a roof of Arab tile. Decomposing, the place mimicked the dead woman's own skeleton: millions of cracks and fissures revealed skeletal bamboo walls, laid bare as the flesh had fallen away. Inside the house were thousands and thousands of filthy undergarments that the old woman had used to cast her spells. Apparently, her favorites were the bloodstained panties of menstruating women. The house smelled rotten. Combined with the humidity, the smells recalled old age.

The body lay upon an improvised table. The dead woman's face appeared to have been painted by an artist with macabre and diabolical inclinations. The stiff body still seemed to evoke panic in those who looked at it. The witch's bristly hair was like that of a small, discolored brush, containing an uneven mixture of black and white. Her eyebrows had disappeared completely. Her sunken eyelids suggested the absence of pupils and eyelashes. Her beak-like nose revealed enormous nostrils that looked much more like grottos for the devil than for dried mucus. Some of her nose hairs had grown long enough to form something like whiskers. Her tarantula mouth was surrounded by velvety growths that resembled hairs. A black sheet covered the witch from her turkey neck to her toes. Beneath the body—on the ground, that is—someone had used lime to paint a large cross.

"The old bat deserved it. All she did was steal air from this world."

"Yes, *comadre,*" her friend answered. "But what has me worried is what she said about that black sheet."

"What?"

"Oh, *comadre.* You mean you never heard?"

"Well, no."

"I can't believe it. Everybody says that her last wish was that her son cover her with that black sheet."

"Really? But what for?"

"They say it was so she could keep on . . . Shh, *comadre,* let's talk about something else. Here comes her son." Then with studied looks they half-smiled at him.

He came over to them and said in a soft voice: *"Comadres,* thank you for coming to be with me." He shook their hands with a brief nod and a somewhat pained expression on his face. After briefly paying his respects, he left.

"So then, *comadre,* what about what you were telling me?"

Hail Mary, full of grace,
the Lord is with thee.
Blessed art thou among women,
and blessed is the
fruit of thy womb, Jesuuuuus.

"Holy Mary, Mother of God, pray for us sinners, now and at the hour of our death. Amen."

Thus were the two gossips interrupted by the *cantora* reciting the rosary for the dead. To avoid looking irreverent, they answered the *cantora's* line—"the fruit of thy womb, Jesuuuuus"—in funereal monotones to complete the prayer.

The rosary prayers continued until the number required for that night had been completed. By the time the *cantora* finished, all of the candles surrounding the body had been lit. As soon as the *cantora* left, the other people slowly went their separate ways. As midnight approached, not a single soul remained, except the witch's son. His pensive face looked like that of an ascetic monk. Every now and then sleep would overcome him and his eyelids would become flaccid, slackening as his eyes blinked.

"*Mamá,*" he said as he began to talk with the dead woman like a sleepy drunk. "Forgive me for not being able to do everything you asked me to do at your death. The truth is that the people who knew you wouldn't give me the chance. Besides, they didn't believe me when I said that you didn't want anyone to see your face after you died. I know that's what you wanted, but please understand that we can't always do everything we're asked."

The entire night went by that way: a monologue with a stone or an inert human. By that time two of the candles had been blown out by sporadic gusts of wind. The stubs remaining on the tin receptacle underneath the body barely helped the incense and the copal continue sending their fragile threads of smoke up to the ceiling.

The next day they carried the body in procession to the cemetery. Never before had the village seen a burial so well attended as this one for the old witch.

"Looks like everybody took the witch's threats seriously," said a woman to an old man.

"Well, why shouldn't they?" he answered. "No matter what they do, they can still hear her threats vibrating in their ears."

"I know. Do you think all those curses she cast upon everybody will come about?"

"Probably."

"Well, I think so, too. Remember, she wasn't wrong about predicting the deaths of Juan Chivo and Secu."

They continued talking in this way. Meanwhile, at the other end of the line, a young girl kept peppering her mother with questions.

"Ma, how come everybody, even Choli the healer, came along with the body today?"

"*Hija*, I told you not to ask so many questions. If you keep this up, you'll find out things that are just for adults. I'll only answer this one question, and then you'll have to be quiet. Understand?"

"Yes."

"Well, a few years ago the witch said that when she died everybody should make sure that she was completely buried; otherwise, she would come back from the grave and kill us all. That's why we're all here: to make sure that she's good and buried."

As they finished talking, they arrived at the edge of the gravesite, which looked much more like a future dam than a grave. As soon as they put the witch into the hole that she herself had excavated years before, everybody—as if by agreement—began to cover her with dirt. The desperation with which they buried her suggested that they were consumed by a desire to see her safely buried many feet under the brown earth. After burying her, they planted a barricade of cedar trees around the grave. They said that they did so to make sure that she couldn't get out even after she became worms, because the cedars' resin would end up chasing her away and back to where she belonged.

When they were finished, they all went home, confident

that the witch had now been relegated to history. Everyone began to live more peacefully, and life seemed to flow smoothly and naturally.

With the passage of time, the witch's drunkard son decided to sell the land where he and his mother had lived for many years. The sale did not seem to go too badly for him. A stranger who specialized in developing village businesses bought the property. Having sold the land, the son found another place to live in town. Having bought new property, the stranger decided to open a tavern. On the very day he opened the tavern, the stranger painted a sign. The tavern was called AQUI ME QUEDO ("I'm Here to Stay").

In back of the tavern, in the very place where the witch had performed her rituals, the tavern owner built a kind of altar. It looked something like a bench in the shape of a cross about a foot-and-a-half above the ground. The owner also planted a maguey cactus close to one of the cross's arms.

As if luck were on the tavern owner's side, the maguey grew large, strong, and healthy. Every fleshy leaf seemed to grow as thick and large as an elephant's trunk.

As the days went by, the tavern got more and more business. All the town's derelicts appeared to have found a fountain of *pulque* in a corner of heaven. From time to time, one woman or another also came into the place. Within the tavern's walls, violence reigned on a daily basis. Every now and always, a brawl would break out among men animated by drink; they would go outside the tavern and exchange gifts of balled fists. After a few kicks and punches, drunken men appeared to be eating tooth soup and warm, red *mole.* A mixture of sweat, spit, snot, and blood flowed from their faces and noses. The loser would stay behind kissing the ground, while the victor would leave triumphant to continue his bohemian life.

After some time, the witch's son began to frequent the tavern (a rather pathetic village saloon, really). At first he went only on Sundays, but soon the tavern became an obsession for him, and he began to go almost every day.

One morning while the drunks were filling their bladders, some young boys went walking around the back of the tavern, near the patio. Because the boys did not have any classes, they decided to have a little fun before going home. One was carrying in his hands a frog of an intensely golden hue. Finding the altar inviting and convenient, the boys sat down. The boy with the tiny golden frog threw his book bag down close to the rustic patio and began to play. He took the frog by the feet and, without letting it go, made it hop as if it were a jumping frog. Then he made it spin around while making the sounds of a helicopter flying by.

"No," said the other boy. "Why don't you give it to me and I'll show you something more fun."

Without objection the first boy handed the frog over to his friend. When the second boy took it, he jammed the frog's haunches into one of the holes in the altar, making the frog look as if it were doing its business on a toilet.

"Well, if that's what you call fun, you'd better give it back to me," complained the first boy.

"All right, if that isn't fun, what do you think about this?" answered the second, and as he finished speaking, he ran one of the maguey's enormous needles through the small frog's fragile head. The poor frog began to die bit by bit, while at the same time its feet twisted helplessly. As the first boy saw what his friend had done, he realized he could do nothing, and he ended up impaling the frog's abdomen on the tip of one of the maguey's thick leaves. Having had their fun, the boys walked away, leaving the frog behind: a sacrificial victim hanging from the maguey.

A couple of hours later, while Lelo, the witch's son, was playing cards with his friends, he got up from his stool, opened the tavern's back window, and spit outside. He finished sucking on a lemon slice he was carrying and threw it out. As he did so, however, he noticed something behind the house.

"Hey, what's that?" he asked his friends, who in turn came over to the window.

"What's what?" All of them tried to look outside to see what he was talking about.

"That thing you can see out there," said Lelo, trying to point with his hand.

"What thing?!"

"That. That thing that looks like a concrete bench."

"Ohhh, that. The owner said he was going to put an altar and a maguey there for good luck."

"An altar?"

"Right. An altar."

"And what saint did he put there to protect it?"

"Well, the Virgin of Guadalupe. But I think he's considering putting another one instead. He just hasn't done it yet because he's afraid of the people around here. Anyway, we told him it would be best not to make the Virgin mad—she might send him straight to hell."

"I see," Lelo responded, returning to the past for a moment. "I can't believe that moron put that thing there. That's the very same place where my mother used to do spells at night. I still remember one night when I found her ripping her entire tongue out. She looked horrible without a tongue and with her mouth open as wide as possible. I also remember how she would make herself throw up into a bedpan and later drink the vomit."

"Lelo, what's going on?"

"Huh?" he answered with a start when one of his friends spoke to him and brought him back to reality.

"Yes, what's going on? All of a sudden you just started babbling like an idiot."

"Oh, it's nothing. It's just that for a second there I was remembering my *vieja.*"

"I see. You miss her, right?" He nodded, but didn't say a word. His friends left the window and abandoned Lelo to his own world.

After a time, Lelo went back to his friends. He played a while longer, drank some shots of *mezcal,* and announced that he had to take a piss. He left the tavern and went around the back. He stopped beside a cedar tree, tried to steady himself on it with one hand, and began to relieve himself between the trunk and the exposed roots. The stream of urine, like hot beer, drew a chaotic zigzag. Lelo was so drunk that he could hardly stay on his feet. It was as if somebody were shaking the ground.

After emptying his bladder, Lelo was in no condition to remember to fasten his belt or zip up his fly. Just as he was about to return to the bar, he staggered to the front of the altar and stood looking at it for a moment. "Ah, *vieja,* the bad part is that I miss you." He began to talk to himself again, almost on the verge of tears. "The good thing is that you're resting now. The bad thing is that the Virgin is with you now. The good thing is that you could learn some new prayers from her and maybe change your life. The bad thing is that she's in your favorite spot now. The good thing is that I'm still with you. But . . . oh, you damned *viejita*, my unlucky *vieja*. Why did you have to leave me so soon?" While he was addressing his mother, Lelo sat down on the altar and burst into tears. He stayed there for a long time, his nose running as he talked and sighed.

"Hey, Lelo, why aren't you coming? What the hell are you doing?"

"Shut up, you mules from hell! Can't you see that I'm talking with my *vieja* for a bit?"

"What *vieja?*"

"My *vieja!* My little mama, may she rest in peace!"

"Well, you're in the wrong place. You're drunk!" They were chiding him even though they could barely stay on their feet themselves. "Don't you know that the dead belong in the cemetery, not in altars? You're the mule."

"So stop screwing around, and give me a moment's peace!"

"It's all right, *compa*, it's all right. Just don't get all hot on us."

They then left Lelo alone, each returning to his own business. "Forgive my idiot friends, *madrecita*; I'm back now." He spent a long time just sitting and looking around as if from somewhere deep within his thoughts something was going to materialize. His entire countenance suggested that of a lost child, as if he did not know how to order his thoughts or recover the ability to think. After a while, he lay down on his side. Because he couldn't get comfortable in that position, he lay down on his back on the altar, fitting his feet, arms, torso, and head in their requisite places along the altar's cross.

Little by little he began to fall asleep. Then, in less time than it takes a cock to crow, he was dead asleep. "It wasn't my fault, I'm telling you. It wasn't," he babbled as he was sleeping and dreaming. "And me? Why am I the one who has to pay? Besides, you're the one who left, and there's nothing left of you there." He spent quite some time in this way, as if he were arguing with an unyielding person.

After a few hours, the drunken spell was broken, and Lelo breathed normally. The day began to disappear as a light, cool mist began to fall. Lelo kept sleeping. The mist became denser. The plants began to be covered by tiny droplets. The entire atmosphere began to sweat. The drunken man, no longer drunk, did not care that his makeshift house had neither roof nor walls; all he wanted was a bed to sleep on.

Meanwhile, the sacrificial frog was getting wetter and wetter. As the mist grew denser, the droplets combined to form ever-larger droplets, some of which began to run. The maguey leaf the frog was impaled on hung right above Lelo's face. Bit by bit the droplets began to fall onto his half-open mouth. From time to time, he moved his lips as if he were tasting the frog-blood water. Just as one of the droplets was about to fall directly into his mouth, a gust of wind blew the droplet off-course, making it land in his nostril. When the drunken man felt the water go into his nose, he awoke, startled.

"Where am I? What am I doing here?" he said as he tried to remember how he had gotten where he was. "Oh, yes, I remember now." He then tried to stand up, but could not. He tried to move his arms, but still he could not. He tried to raise his head and turn it, but he soon realized that he was like a half-paralyzed zombie. He could feel everything; in particular, he could easily feel the mist falling on his skin, but he could not move most of his body. The only parts he could move were his eyes, his tongue, and his mouth. Worse, even though he could move his mouth, he could not cry out. His thorax, however, moved as he inhaled or exhaled.

Again and again he tried to move, but without success. Eventually he began to feel that his tongue was growing more and more numb. He tried to see if he could open his mouth. He opened it. Unfortunately, after opening his mouth he could not close it. His mouth widened so much that it felt like an invisible force were separating his upper and lower jaws. No matter how he fought to close his mouth, he remained in the pose of a starving man begging for food. Because he could not move, he continued to lie on his back and look up to the heavens, thinking about everything that might happen to him. He never imagined, though, what was actually coming. Gradually he began to focus his eyes on things that were closer to him, until they came to rest on the small frog impaled on the maguey needle. As he studied the frog, he realized that a droplet was about to fall directly into his mouth.

"No. No. I have to close my mouth before that damned water falls in," he thought to himself as he furiously fought to close his mouth.

The problem was that the droplet, stretched by the force

of gravity and its own potential energy, allowed itself to fall softly and simply onto the man's exposed palate. Lelo tried to spit it out, but failed; more than anything, he sounded as if he were trying to cough gobs of mucus out of his throat. Whether he wanted it or not, the droplet formed part of his saliva. His throat's reflexes made him swallow the saliva. After only a few brief seconds, another droplet fell into the same grave of living flesh. At this point the poor man was desperate to close his mouth. Not only could he not close his mouth, but he could not cry, shout, or blink. And so Lelo's torture went on.

Nevertheless, something worse was yet to come. Because the condensation made everything perspire, the impaled frog's flesh began to soften. The man saw that all that moisture was making the inert little body of the golden frog, the defenseless amphibian, begin to slip. Even as the man battled to close his mouth, the frog fell directly on target. The man made gagging noises with his mouth, struggling to expel the tiny dead body. After many unsuccessful attempts, he had to rest. He could sense how the frog's gastric juices, muscles, and skin layers introduced themselves into his unprotected throat. Then, still lying there, Lelo felt something moving along his pants over his calf.

"What's that? Please, somebody help me!"

Little by little he began to feel something introducing itself in slow motion under his clothes. Chills ran through him, but still he could not move. The animal continued to advance; as it did so, Lelo began to sense that a hand, hairy and spiny, was scratching against his skin. He felt that the animal genuinely knew that he could do nothing and was exploiting his powerlessness. It crossed his ankle. It crossed his knee. It traversed the entire length of his thigh. Soon it arrived at a point just below his pelvis. It stopped for a moment, as if it were trying to decide where to go.

After a few seconds, seconds that seemed like an eternity to Lelo, the animal began its hairy journey once again. Instead of continuing upward, however, it took a slight detour and explored what was between Lelo's legs. It traipsed all over Mount Venus. Not finding anything blocking its path, it began moving again toward the navel. Finally, the animal left that area, crossing the navel, the abdomen, and the chest. When the animal reached the throat, the man could finally see that it was an enormous spider. He felt that it was at least the size of a fist. Wanting to avoid tiring itself out, the spider did not climb over the chin; instead, it crawled over one of Lelo's temples, crossed over to the ear, stood there a bit, and then perched between the nose and the open mouth.

"No, Blessed Virgin, no! It's a massive tarantula!" shouted the man in silence as he watched the creature from the corner of his eye.

The tarantula never stopped moving its feet; it looked as if it were playing a piano made of flesh. It began wandering slowly between the mouth and the nose and from one cheek to the other. The man watched every single movement it made. His breathing became more labored, sonorous. He no longer wanted to move. What he wanted more than anything else was to close his mouth. As if having read Lelo's thoughts and taken them as an invitation, the spider began to crawl into the gaping mouth. Lelo could feel how the spider's feet dug into his lips like tweezers. He could also sense how the spider made its way along his teeth, his tongue, and his palate.

For only a brief moment, the tarantula probed the man's saliva. Then, for some reason, the creature decided to continue its journey down the throat. The man was nearly suffocating: he could neither speak nor cry out.

"Lelo!" his friends shouted again from the tavern window. They waited a few seconds to see if there was any reaction.

"Help me! For God's sake, help me!" Lelo cried out in his thoughts.

"It looks like he's fallen asleep. He looks so calm and peaceful," noted one of the men.

"No, I'm not asleep!"

"That's enough. Stop bugging him," said another. "Let him stay there sleeping with his mother." Having said their piece, Lelo's friends left the window and went back to their drinking.

"Nooooooo! Don't goooooo! Get me out of here!" shouted the unfortunate man, as if he were buried in a tomb or in a cave where no one could hear him. He tried everything he could to move some part of his body. Then, as if by some miracle, he managed to move his jaw, but not his lips or his tongue. When he tried to move his mouth to get the tarantula out, however, his mouth snapped hermetically shut: he could not open it again. When the spider felt the pressure from the mouth, it began to bite everything in its path. It left several bites at the base of the tongue, then started tearing desperately at the uvula and the epiglottis, struggling to break through. The man felt as if something were ripping his throat raw.

By the time the spider had gone about halfway down his throat, the man was near death. He struggled and fought for air. He began to have convulsions in his chest and stomach. He looked as if he were suffering from a bizarre case of the hiccups. Because of the massive contractions in his diaphragm, his dying chest appeared to be leaping out of him.

Suddenly, as if by a miracle, the man was able to open his mouth again. Unfortunately, the tarantula kept moving down his throat. The man continued breathing slowly, well aware of every step, every prick of the hellish spider.

And so, with his mouth agape, whether because of the pain, the venom, or the lack of oxygen, he fainted in terror.

"Oh, blessed Virgin in heaven," exclaimed an older woman, crossing herself as she looked at the recently discovered body. "The poor thing must have drunk too much."

"I think so, too, *comadre,*" answered another.

"No. I think that filthy witch took him with her black magic," interrupted an elderly man, who had come to see the body after its discovery earlier that morning. The lifeless face had several water droplets on it, as if even in death the man were still sweating.

"You really think so?" asked one of the *comadres.*

"Of course," answered the man. "Don't you remember how her face looked like a tarantula when she died?"

"Oh. Well then, yes. Didn't I tell you, *comadre,* that her disgusting witchcraft hadn't left the village?" In the same vein they continued proposing different theories as they looked over the rigid body.

Translated by Daryl R. Hague

She Has Reddish Hair and Her Name Is Sabina

Julieta Campos

I MUST LEAVE. Many have gone to eat but others are arriving, some for the first time because they have scarcely gotten themselves registered in the hotel and do not want to waste the rest of the day, and so they put on swimsuits to go down to the pool and take advantage of even half an hour before coming up to the dining room; others, because they have already eaten and felt too lonely in their rooms and told themselves they did not come here for this, and

JULIETA CAMPOS (1932–) was born in Cuba and has lived in Mexico City since 1955. She has worked as a translator, editor, and the director of the Mexico chapter of PEN. She has published several books about Mexico's indigenous communities and numerous novels, including *Muerte por el agua* (1965) and *La forza del destino* (2004). Several of her novels have been published in English, including *The Fear of Losing Eurydice* (1993), and a collection of her short stories, *Celina or the Cats*, was published in 1995. This excerpt is taken from *She Has Red Hair and Her Name is Sabina* (1993), winner of the Xavier Villaurrutia Prize. The novel is set in a single moment on a balcony in Acapulco. Sabina is a character in the mind of the novel's narrator.

that it's better down there and preferable to take their siestas protected by the umbrella, allowing themselves to doze
through the chattering and the sound the water makes
when someone dives into the pool. There are no children
at this hour. Of course they are taking their siestas in their
rooms and later on will awaken as if it were another day
and go running down to the ocean cove because there are
crabs there, and seashells, fish, and even little starfish fas-
tened against the rocks coated with a slippery green that
makes one a little fearful about touching them. Yesterday
or the day before, when it had gotten dark and they turned
on the spotlights that illuminate the promontory between
seven and ten, when I sat here as I do every night to contemplate the scenery so often deserted at this hour, I realized a girl was down there, almost an adolescent, slipping
between the ropes that separate the cement deck built over
the rocks that encircle the cove and divide it from the outer
rocks and the ocean which is nonetheless constantly leaping over the strands to sweep over the platform and occasionally climb up some of the steps leading to the promontory. The child is completely alone and there is a sort of
defiance in her game, an ingenuous, spontaneous defiance,
perhaps heedlessness, toward the violence of the waves. I
am on the point of shouting at her or going down to warn
her of the danger, but I don't do it. It seems to me, I don't
know why, that I have no right to interrupt her, that in her
willful and provocative loneliness she is acting out a ritual
game in order to make her free from something. It is a privilege to watch her playing her solitary game, like the rep-
etition of an ancestral rite which she is observing without
being aware of it. When you, when I, saw her, her gesture

was saved and would not be lost. Why those shouts? Why those voices? Why the stubbornness about remembering implacably that I ought to remember? I am the one seated on the pier, twenty-two years ago. The four-o'clock light is merciless. It isn't true that there is a story to tell. Now they are impatient. They have already closed the suitcases but have not decided to leave the air-conditioned room. They open the door just a bit to prevent the heat from slipping in, and they shout at you without being able to explain to themselves why you remain there as if you didn't hear them. The voices sound muffled in the heat, as if someone were speaking inside a bottle containing another that contains still another. The light is greenish, moonlike, as in a strange nocturnal dawn. The light is too white and can split you in two as an arrow does an apple. The light is yellow like a moving picture filmed in sepia and it leaves the two of them under a spell, characters in a book that is not this one, butterflies within an oval frame. The light is amber in the room with the leaded glass where two little girls are pretending to play, are levitating as if they were playing, posing as if they were playing, pretending the air does not smell like rotten ferns. There are no ghosts at four in the afternoon. Anything can happen.

Translated by Leland H. Chambers

Vigil in Tehuantepec

Alberto Ruy Sánchez

A HOARSE AND DELIBERATE VOICE slowly woke me. At first I didn't know what it was saying. The deep grain of that voice was disturbing my dreams, devouring them, mixing with them, making them disappear in the confusion of its whirlwind. Little by little I started to realize that it was coming from the corridor facing my window. It was a kind of long balcony over the patio facing all of the rooms of the Oasis Hotel. The heat reached up to my face in waves, as if every time someone walked on the patio they pushed dense air toward us, an oven door opening in front of us. The voice was directed toward another man, who was

---

ALBERTO RUY SÁNCHEZ (1951–) was born and lives in Mexico City, where he is editor-in-chief of *Artes de México* magazine. For eight years he lived in France, where he received a doctorate from the University of Paris. His novel, *Los nombres del aire* (1987), won the Xavier Villaurrutia Prize and was translated into English as *Mogador* (1992). He is also the author of *En los labios del agua* (1996) and *Los jardines secretos de Mogador* (2001). He has been awarded a Guggenheim fellowship and the French government's Order of Arts and Letters.

---

listening in near silence, immersed in that story, just as I was suddenly starting to be:

"They hung them by their feet from the big tree in the plaza, the one that fills with white sweet-smelling flowers every year. Since so many people had beaten them, their blood stained all of the flowers when they were hung. From a distance, it looked like a family of jaguars had climbed the tree and was waiting to eat the outlaws. Even though they were already more dead than alive, they still let out a few screams of pain from some corner of hell. Then they were castrated and set on fire. Half of the tree burned all day and part of the night, the flames engulfing all of the flowers. The smell remained stuck in the air for several months and all of us carried it on our persons despite how often we bathed. We smelled like burned garbage, but worse. Suddenly, the smell of the flowers and the sweet sap of the tree would mix together. At first it was very disgusting, but later it was pleasant from time to time."

When I could, I got up and opened the venetian blind. There was no one in the corridor. Magui woke up at that moment and I asked her if she too had heard the story.

"You were dreaming," she affirmed, smiling.

But I seriously doubted it, remembering that on several prior occasions I had had mixed feelings and dreams.

We had arrived in Tehuantepec at night, very late and very tired from a trip along a dry, long, and winding path. For several hours the road slid between the hills like a black snake between ocher-colored dirt and yellow rocks. Tonight one of the most anticipated feasts is celebrated in Tehuantepec—a "vigil"—and the two hotels in town are filled. We found two rooms in the Oasis Hotel because it is owned by the family of a friend of our traveling companion, Margarita Dalton, the director of the Instituto de Cultura in Oaxaca. Her friend is the director of the Casa de la Cultura in Tehuantepec. Later, Magui and Margarita will go with her so that she can lend them traditional *tehuana* dresses; no woman can attend the vigil if she isn't wearing the traditional dress: several entangled layers of petticoats over large rear ends and a wide lace border almost reaching to the ground. A plain sleeveless blouse *a la Andalusia* called *huipil corto* and is covered with embroidered flowers, like the skirt. On the head and falling onto the shoulders and back is an enclosed section of white lace like a skirt that is called *huipil largo*. At mass it's worn in such a way that one's face is completely concealed, like a white aura, and on the street, in a different way, more open. It's the dress that Frida Kahlo is wearing so often in photographs because she adopted it as the uniform of her public persona. In the 1940s and '50s the *tehuana* was the symbol of a romantic vision of Mexico. The myth of a matriarchal society nurtured that symbol. Sergei Eisenstein believed this in 1932 and one of the chapters of *Que viva México* was dedicated to the *tehuanas*. It was called *Zandunga*, like the traditional wedding song. It portrays a seminude woman sleeping in the hammock while a man does the house and field work.

In fact, *tehuanas* and *juchitecas* exhibit a markedly bold personality. Their body language expresses more self-confidence and their relations with men are more active. Beginning with their amorous courtship, the *tehuana* looks and touches and says whatever she wants to. Furthermore, the beauty of the women of the Isthmus of Tehuantepec is one of their certainties.

Traditionally, they dedicate themselves to business and the men to fieldwork. They handle the money, and, together, domestic and community life. A legendary woman named Doña Juana Catalina is the heroine of Isthmus identity. Almost a century ago she was a kind of political boss of the region. Her house, an emphatically capital-like residence located in a small, rural city setting, rises uniquely near the train tracks and next to the market as a symbol of its economic and political power. Her loving bond with Porfirio Díaz has eclipsed her role as an advocate and leader of her region. People say that at the beginning of the public festivities she established the rules of the traditional dress, the headdress, and the jewelry that should always be worn: a gold coin necklace with the peculiar earrings, and, on one's head, ribbons and braids intertwined to form a semicircle. The jewelry is purchased or rented for the feasts at a special market stand, between the sandals and the baskets. Dead for several generations, Doña Juana Catalina is present at all the feasts by virtue of the strict observance of her rules.

Dawn arrives early in Tehuantepec. While the others wake up, Magui and I go out to explore the streets to see how the people here go about planning the beginning of their day. While we were leaving our room we realized that it was covered from the floor to the ceiling with glazed tiles, including the bed and the shelves. It gives you the impression that it's cleaned by spraying water from a hose. Only the sheets and the mattress have to be removed. It's refreshing and it could be hygienic, although with the tremendous heat that exists here, sweat surely condenses on the ceiling drop by drop during nights of excited love-making. It's now dawn and the heat and humidity are already everywhere. The sea is very close by, but not close enough for us to see it from where we are. But it does arrive in the air with the waves of heat. We're on one of the streets of the market and the central plaza, filled with trees. I instinctively look for a tree that is burned and I find an immense one that is missing a section. Could it be the one from the story I heard in the confusion of my dreams? The plaza is full of flowers. The market surrounds it on two sides and the municipal office of the president on a third. It seems to be in a state of reconstructed ruins; there are half-built walls and the enormous back patio where the feast is going to be held is no longer surrounded by anything. Later in the day it will be closed off by a wire fence.

Walking toward the market we see the women coming and going with their shopping baskets. They almost always wear their hair loose and have an arrogant way of walking. One of them passes in front of us like a mythological being on a moving cloud. She is standing immobile on the back part of a small battery-charged motorcycle. It's like a roman chariot without horses on which she is supporting herself with one hand, proud, with her face into the wind.

Suddenly, another chariot appears and then another among a cluster of people walking. We discover that they're taxis with three wheels that the women hire when they exit the market. Some of them are carrying two passengers with their baskets at their feet. A multitude of chariots appears at the corner. They float back and forth in the air without moving. The drivers almost can't be seen because they're in the front, inside a small cabin. No automobiles appear to contend for the street with the flying or walking *tehuanas*. Their presence is imposing, strange, and hypnotic.

We arrive at a juice stand at the outer edge of the market, in front of the plaza. There is a counter and five tall stools. We calmly sit down to wait for the juices we ordered: a guava, a pineapple, and a mango. The noise of the chariots could be heard clearly. But in the background, very far away, another sound could also be heard; it was like an orchestra of distorted breathing sounds, coming from a distant radio. After observing us mistakenly pondering the sound, Zumero the bartender explained: "That noise comes from the Pan-American road. It's the horns of the big cargo trucks. Only one road that comes from South America crosses Central America and unites the north with the entire subcontinent. And it goes by Tehuantepec."

"Do they always blow their horns when they go by here?"

The bartender laughs at me before slowly responding: "No, it just so happens that they're blowing their horns because they can't pass. The road is blocked. . . ."

He was going to tell us something else when a truck filled with soldiers entered the plaza. It drove up to the edge of the market and then they descended, making tremendous noise with their boots, and entered. Another truck arrived immediately and did the same.

"What's happening over there?"

"Well, nothing, what always happens in these cases. They're going to lynch them."

"Who is going to be lynched?"

"The thieves. And together with them the three police-men from the township who tried to remove them and supposedly take them to jail, surely to set them free with a big or small *mordida* as payment. At the moment they've already received a good beating. Here the people ask for and carry out justice when the police fail them. The taxi drivers are blocking the streets leading into town and closed the Pan-American. And to top it off, the soldiers come to protect the thieves. How disgraceful. Everything is upside down."

A mob rushed out of the center of the market. The women were hitting the soldiers with everything they had in their hands. The policemen, with their uniforms torn to pieces, were covering their heads and faces with their arms and trying to position themselves behind the soldiers. In that galaxy of blows that was coming toward us, the two thieves looked like a pair of old bloody rags that everyone was carrying off. Finally, the people took one of the thieves to the market again and locked him in a kind of wire cage that was used as a bodega. The soldiers took the other one and locked him in the town hall office.

A very short woman with a thunderous voice suddenly appeared among the crowd and ordered everyone to be quiet. The silence made her bigger. They let her say six sentences and then the shouting, the anger, and the insults started again. None of the factions was willing to give up their part of the human spoils of war.

In the middle of the simultaneous shouting, the little president no longer knew who to listen to and gave the order that the townspeople decide right then and there who their representatives were because she couldn't talk to everyone at the same time. "Also decide what you want to attain. Because you're not going to kill them just like that. That's not going to happen here again. We're not animals."

It was then I seemed to understand what the man who had unintentionally woke me up in the morning was talking about. The bartender clarified it for us: "Yes, it was exactly a year ago, the day of the vigil, when other thieves who weren't from here (they always come from other towns) wanted to rob the jewelry stand in the market. They were greatly tempted by allowing themselves to be impressed by so much gold jewelry dangling off the women. Later, they spotted a small stand in the market and it was easy for them. The people beat them badly, castrated them, doused them in gasoline, and while they were hanging, still alive, set them on fire."

I pointed out the half tree that I had seen.

"No, that was from another year. About seven trees have been burned in the plaza over the last twenty years, some of them several times. The good thing is that with this sun and this humidity everything grows again. The plaza was no longer open then. That one was from last year."

He pointed out a very large tree without any trace of fire or lynchings, filled with white flowers.

"It's true," he further clarified, "that when someone has been hung from a tree the young women from here absolutely do not want any of its flowers in their hair. They say that the flowers give them bad luck and then steal their boyfriends."

The president quickly walked by next to us, the only strangers in the plaza, and asked us if we were journalists. When we told her no, she seemed relieved and walked away without saying good-bye. Three steps later she called over an assistant and gave him an order: "Take those Guatemalans to the Casa de Cultura and entertain them there with speeches and dancing. Stage something for them that will keep them quiet, so that they don't notice anything."

I asked our bartender who were those Guatemalans that they were going to distract. I hoped that he didn't think it was us.

"It's a group of twenty municipal officials from Guatemala who are here for a conference, invited by the Oaxaca government."

"And are they going to be able to conceal that?"

"Yes, the people who don't know, don't know. At most they're going to believe that there's a little bit of disorder. And seeing so many soldiers shouldn't be rare to them. They say that over there there are even more soldiers in the street. The bad thing is that at the very beginning of the robbery someone spread the rumor that the thieves had been Guatemalans. There were already many people carrying sticks and torches heading for their hotel when a few taxi drivers grabbed the real thieves in the roadblock and brought them to the market. I don't know if you've noticed, but there are no other strangers here today, except you, the Guatemalans, and the thieves. The road has been closed and no one can enter or leave, not even the tourists who want to come to the feast."

Magui and I spent the entire day walking around the city. The market was our destination, but we also visited the house of Doña Juana Catalina, which was shown to us by her granddaughter, who is already a young grandmother.

The furniture of a century ago occupies the same space; like ghosts, the chairs talk about a distant pleasure, forgotten conversations, incoherent legends. We visit the Santo Domingo convent, which is the Casa de Cultura, and walk through the neighborhoods, each one with its own small church. The preparations for the feast continue everywhere. Each neighborhood will present their queen at night and the orchestras are rehearsing their tunes. Here and there, all over town, one can hear passages of the song that identifies everyone as if it were a regional hymn: "Zandunga."

But we also see traces of the possible lynching everywhere. Everyone talks about it and from time to time one can hear or see mobs running from one place to another. And the negotiations with the president shift from one place to another throughout the entire small city to escape from the Guatemalans, like in a comedy of errors. Everyone was helping. It was like hiding an elephant in an anthill with all of the ants pretending that they don't see anything, and apparently they were being successful. The feast served to justify all the anomalies. A lady from Guatemala was at the market buying that traditional cheese from Oaxaca they call *quesillo* and is like a long, narrow strip of white strings wrapped around each other many times forming a ball. In conversation the president told her that the explanations she was being given about the chaos weren't very logical. For example, the cars stopped in traffic. It seemed to her that that didn't help the feast preparations but rather impeded them. The woman who bought the cheese simply replied: "That's the way they are in Oaxaca. In what other place in the world is even cheese rolled up?"

In the afternoon the line of cars and trucks on the road very likely extended for several kilometers. Some said twenty; others said fifty. The truth is that the scandal that was coming from that side of the horizon was worsening as the day progressed just as much as the heat, which was constant. Our obsessive thinking was naturally about a good hammock for the siesta. Heat devours people; it drains their energy. People are the product of those who nourish themselves to continue growing until they get indigestion and close their eyes. But at night the heat doesn't decrease, it remains quiet, blind, invisible, always tactile.

But the feast begins and all of the faces become illuminated. The women, proud of their beauty and their dresses, are on parade at all times. The dress transforms the *tehuana* into the center of the world. Or makes the fact that she is more evident. Covered with embroidered flowers that sprout from the fabric is a garden, the garden of gardens. When she moves it's a promise of paradise. Her dowry of gold coins announces her central position in the community, power, and is a symbol of both. By the golden splendor of her appearance one presumes that she is the axis of courting, of coquetry, of the preludes of love life. Her hairstyle and makeup—with the preeminence of the eyes— reveal their dominion over the codes of appearance. The men are scrupulously dressed in white shirts and dark pants, some with sombreros and brightly colored neckerchiefs around their necks. The head of each family presents himself before the table of the majordomo, who is in charge of organizing the feast, with a carton of beer; a symbolic participation in the expenses of the community, an indication of belonging to everyone's feast. The Isthmus *son* is a slow dance of smooth and elegant movements. The dance partners perform the rituals of initiating the dance. The men look small and fragile. The women frequently dance among themselves, bringing their voluminous waists together. The several layers of petticoats cause the skirt to make the body bulkier. Being thin is synonymous with ugliness. The grandmothers dance with their granddaughters, the daughters with their sisters. The feet can't be seen because the dress almost drags on the floor. Small paper banners are inserted into the headdresses. The most voluminous women move smoothly, like transatlantic liners maneuvering on the dance floor as if in a port.

At dawn we learned that the taxi drivers' strike had ended and everyone had reached an agreement. The president entered the feast steadfastly with a smile as wide as her leadership ability. She is dressed for the feast. Everyone greets her, entertains her. She sits down at the head table like a King Solomon of the tropics and the desert. But the real queen of the feast was coronated hours before. Her entourage is the queens of each neighborhood. They have placed an elevated throne behind the dance floor for her, from which she watches all the activities of the feast with her shiny crown and her scepter in her right hand.

The truck drivers who had been stopped on the road all day angrily invade the city driving only the front part of their trucks. They make an indescribable noise with their horns and motors. There are more than twenty that surround the patio where we are celebrating and they drive round and round us. Every now and then they blow the same tune with their horns; it's one that is very well known in Mexico as an insult, which sings out: *¡chinga tu madre!*

To say that insult is to lambaste someone. No one at the feast gets the message and they continue dancing as if nothing was happening. A lady next to me says: "We've been lambasted, but with this heat it's even appreciated. There isn't even rain for this feast."

Since the truck drivers continue making noise that is also soothing, the president gives the order to raise the volume of the music. The horns vibrate. The glasses on the table, also. The sound is felt on the body as if something were touching us. A brusque massage of vibrations. But the people keep dancing as if nothing were wrong. The excess of this touching music turns into a type of rapture for everyone. The slow pace of the feast quickens in the midst of the threat of aggression by the truck drivers and a new orchestra, more modern, goes into action.

The truck drivers stop suddenly to look at the three singers of the new orchestra in their little shiny bikinis. Later they drive around a few more times in their vehicles of immense wheels and disappear as if they had been dissolved in the tremendous and chaotic noise they favored. Many people don't even notice that they've left. When the windows of a house nearby shatter, someone decides to lower the volume of the music. Some say that the feast is called a vigil because no one sleeps; we all stay awake the entire night. Others say it's because of the *cirio*, a mourner's candle that is offered to the patron of the town, neighborhood, or association during the feast. In any case, the appearance of the sun extinguishes all the candles. The sun takes us by surprise while we're dancing. Magui wants us to take a stroll underneath the sweet-smelling trees of the plaza before returning to the hotel. The chariots and their crew members are still sleeping. The market slowly starts to come to life. A few youngsters go directly from the feast to open their vegetable or flower stands.

We seem to spot a burned tree at the furthest edge of the plaza. One can see that it was from last night and that it was extinguished with dirt and water. It's useless to ask what happened; no one knows, no one will say anything. Stains that might be of blood and oil are perceived under the dirt thrown on top of the cobblestones of the plaza and on some white flowers with absorbent petals. Even the bartender at the juice stand shows himself to be incisive and evasive: "Nothing happened here. Well, yes, there was a feast. Who didn't go to the vigil?"

Translated by Harry Morales

Tenebrae Service

Rosario Castellanos

SAINT JOHN THE PROTECTOR, the one who was present when the worlds first appeared, the one who gave approval for the century to begin, one of the pillars that holds firm that which is firm, Saint John the Protector looked down one day to contemplate the world of men.

His eyes went from the sea where the fishes play to the mountain where the snow sleeps. They passed over the plain where the wind mounts its fury, over the beaches of

---

ROSARIO CASTELLANOS (1925–74) was born in Mexico City, the daughter of a wealthy landowner from Chiapas. She grew up in Chiapas, in the remote town of Comitán de las Flores and her family's even more remote Hacienda de El Rosario. In the late 1930s, after losing much of their land in the reforms of President Cardenas, the family came to Mexico City. Poet, novelist, essayist, journalist, and diplomat, she was one of Mexico's most distinguished literary personalities. She was in Tel Aviv, serving as Mexico's ambassador to Israel, when she was electrocuted in a household accident. Her works available in English are *The Nine Guardians* (1959), *Another Way to Be: Selected Works of Rosario Castellanos* (1990), and *The Book of Lamentations* (1996).

---

shimmering sand, over the forests made for the animals' cautious roaming, over the valleys.

The gaze of Saint John the Protector fell upon the valley that is called Chamula. He was pleased with the softness of the hills as they came breathlessly from afar to seek repose here. He was pleased with the nearness of the sky, and with the morning fog. And it was then that the spirit of Saint John was moved with the desire to be revered in this place. And so that there would be no lack of material for the building of the church and so that the church would be white, Saint John turned all the white sheep of all the flocks grazing there into stones.

The promontory, silent and motionless, remained there as a sign of good will. But the tribes that populated the valley of Chamula, the Tzotzil bat-men, did not know how to interpret the sign. Not even the elders, nor the men of the council, were able to offer a valid opinion. All was confused muttering, downcast eyes, arms failing in fearful gesturing. Because of this, other men had to come later. And these men came as if from another world. The sun was in their faces and they spoke in a haughty tongue, a tongue that strikes fear into the hearts of those who hear it. A language, not like the Tzotzil, which is spoken also in dreams, but instead an iron instrument of lordship, a weapon of conquest, the sharp scourge of the law. Because how, if not in Castilian, are orders given and sentences declared? And how is it possible to punish and reward if not in Castilian?

But not even the new arrivals understood exactly the enigma of the petrified sheep. They only understood the command that gives orders to work. And they with their heads, and the Indians with their hands, began the construction of a temple. By day they dug a ditch for cement, but by night the ditch became level. By day they raised the wall, and by night the wall fell. Saint John the Protector had to come in person, pushing the rocks himself, one by one, making them roll down the slopes until they were all gathered in the place where they were to remain. Only then did the efforts of the men achieve their reward.

The building is white, just as Saint John the Protector wanted it to be. And since that time the consecrated air above the altar resounds with the prayers and the songs of the white *caxlán*, the laments and supplications of the Indian. The wax burns in total immolation of itself; the incense exhales its fervent soul; the cypress boughs refresh and perfume the air. And from the most eminent niche of the main altar the image of Saint John the Protector (finely silhouetted in polychromed wood) keeps watch over the other images: Saint Margaret with her tiny feet, the giver of gifts; Saint Augustine, robust and serene; Saint Geronimo, with the tiger in his entrails, secret protector of witches; Our Lady of Sorrows, with a storm cloud reddening her horizon; the enormous cross of Good Friday, demanding its annual victim, poised as if on the brink of crashing down like a catastrophe. Hostile powers that had to be restrained so as not to unleash their forces. Anonymous virgins, mutilated apostles, unwieldy angels tumbled in turn from altar to bier and to the floor, where they then fell prostrate. Matter without virtue, which piety forgets and oblivion disdains. Unhearing ear, indifferent breast, closed hand.

And that is the way things were said to have happened from the beginning. It is true. There are testimonies. They can be read on the arches of the door at the entrance to the temple, from whence the sun bids its farewells.

This place is the center. The three communities of Chamula surround it: the seat of government, the religious and political center, and the ceremonial city.

To Chamula the Indian dignitaries come from the most remote places in the highlands of Chiapas, where Tzotzil is spoken. Here they receive their assignments.

The office with the greatest responsibility is that of president and, next to it, that of scribe. They are assisted by mayors, aldermen, elders, governors, and alms-keepers. There are stewards who are entrusted with the care of the saintly images and ensigns to organize the sacred festivals. These "passions" are set during Carnival week.

The assignments last twelve months, and the officers, transitory inhabitants of Chamula, occupy the huts scattered across the hills and plains, supporting themselves by working the land, raising farm animals, and tending herds of sheep.

Upon the conclusion of the term, the representatives, bestowed with dignity and honor, return to their villages. They then enjoy the status of former authorities. They spent many hours in deliberation with their president, and the deliberations were reported in the written record, on "paper that speaks," by the scribe. They settled matters of boundaries, abolished rivalries, established justice, tied and untied marriage unions. And, most important, they were privileged to serve the divine. It was entrusted to their care for vigilant protection and reverence. And thus the chosen ones, the flower of the race, are not permitted to enter the divine presence during the day with work-feet but rather

with prayer-feet. Before beginning any task, before pro-
nouncing any word, the man who serves as an example to
the others must prostrate himself before his father, the sun.

The sun rises late in Chamula. The rooster crows to dis-
perse the fog. Slowly the men stretch. Slowly the women
stoop and blow the ashes to uncover the faces of the coals.
Around the hut the wind roams. And under the thatched
roof and between the four walls made of mud, the cold air
is the guest of honor.

Pedro González Winikton separated his hands, which
meditation had joined together, and let them fall at his
sides. He was an Indian of great stature and firm muscles.
Despite his youth (that premature, severe youth typical of
his race) others came to him as if he were an elder brother.
The accuracy of his decisions, the zeal of his commands, the
purity of his customs, gave him a certain status among the
respected people, and only in the execution of his duties did
his heart sing within him. And so, when it fell his lot to
accept the investiture of judge, and when he took his vows
before the cross in the atrium of the Church of Saint John,
he was happy. His wife, Catalina Díaz Puiljá, wove a garment out of thick, black wool that covered him fully to the
knee. So that he would be highly regarded in the assembly.

Therefore, as of December 31 of that year, Pedro
González Winikton and Catalina Díaz Puiljá established
themselves in Chamula. They were given a hut in which to
live and a plot of ground to farm. The maize field was
there, already green, promising a bountiful harvest. What
more could Pedro desire if he already had material abundance, prestige among his equals, the devotion of his wife?
Unable to express his deep satisfaction, the smile on his

face endured for an instant. His countenance again became rigid. Winikton thought of himself as a hollow stalk, the stubble that is burned after the harvest. He also compared himself to a weed. Because he had no children.

Catalina Díaz Puiljá, barely twenty years old but already withered and tired, was given to Pedro by her parents when she was still a child. The early days were happy. The lack of issue was viewed as normal. But later, when the companions with whom Catalina spun yarn and gathered water and wood began to walk a little more heavily (because they carried both themselves and the ones to come), when their eyes became peaceful and their wombs began to swell like full granaries, then Catalina felt her fruitless hips, cursed the lightness of her step, and, suddenly turning to look behind her, found that she left no footprints. And she felt anguish thinking that her name would pass from the memory of her village in the same way. And from then on she could not rest.

She consulted with the elders, thrust her pulse to the ears of the soothsayers. They investigated the circulation of her blood, gathered facts, consulted among themselves. Where did your road turn, Catalina? Where did you go astray? Where was your spirit made afraid? Catalina sweated, overcome by the vapor of the miraculous herbs. She did not know how to respond. And her moon did not turn white like those of women who can conceive, but it was dyed red like the moon of single women and widows. Like the moon of the women of pleasure.

Then the pilgrimage began. She went on to the *custi-taleros*, the wandering people who were always informed of the latest news from afar. And in the deepest recesses of their minds they kept the names of the places she needed to visit. In Cancuc there was an old woman who served as a spell-caster or as a sorceress, depending on how she was needed. In Biqu'it Bautista a witch probed the depths of the night to interpret its designs. In Tenejapa lived a witch doctor of excellent reputation. Catalina sought advice from them all, bearing her humble gifts: the first tender ears of corn, large carafes of liquor, a baby lamb.

And so, for Catalina the light of hope began to grow dim, and she shut herself away in a somber world ruled by arbitrary forces. And she learned to appease these forces when they were adverse, to encourage them when they were propitious, to manipulate their portent. She repeated brutalizing litanies. Deliriously she ran through flames of fire without being harmed. She had now become one of those who dared to look mystery straight in the eye. An *ilol* in whose lap rest many spells. Anyone she looked upon with a frown would tremble; anyone she smiled upon felt relief. But Catalina's womb was still closed. Closed as tight as a nut.

Out of the corner of her eye, as she knelt before the stone to grind the day's ration of meal, Catalina studied the silhouette of her husband. When would he repudiate her? How long would he endure the insult of her sterility? Marriages like theirs were customarily thought invalid. One word from Winikton would be enough to send her back to her family's hut in Tzajal-hemel. She would no longer find her father there, for he had died years before. She would no longer find her mother there, as she too had passed on. The only one left was her brother Lorenzo, known to all as *"el inocente"* because of his simplemindedness and the empty laugh that distorted his face.

Catalina stood up and put the ball of dough in her husband's knapsack. What kept him with her? Fear? Love? Winikton's face hid his secret well. Without a gesture of farewell, the man left the hut. The door closed behind him.

An irrevocable decision froze Catalina's countenance. She would never allow a separation; she refused to be left alone; she would not be publicly humiliated!

Her movements became more lively, as if she were fighting an adversary then and there. She moved about her hut, guiding herself more by touch than by sight, since the light penetrated only through the holes in the wall, and the room was darkened, filled with smoke. Even more than touch, habit directed her movements, keeping her from knocking over the objects that were piled up haphazardly in the cramped space. Pots of clay, chipped and broken, the grinding stone—too new, not yet dominated by the strength and ability of the grinder—tree trunks instead of chairs, ancient chests with broken locks. And, reclined against the fragile sides of the hut, innumerable crosses—a wooden one whose towering height seemed to uphold the walls, the others of intertwined palm leaves, small and butterfly-like. Hanging from the central cross were the initials of Pedro González Winikton, Judge. And scattered on the floor were the tools of trade of Catalina Díaz Puiljá, Weaver.

The murmur of activity coming from the other huts, increasingly distinct and pressing, made Catalina shake her head as if to scare away a bad dream that tormented her. She hurried to complete her preparations. In a net she carefully placed the eggs gathered from a nest the night before, wrapped in leaves to avoid their breaking. When the net was full, Catalina carried it on her back. The leather band that dug into her forehead gave the impression of a deep scar.

A group of women had gathered around the hut in silence to await Catalina's appearance. One by one they paraded in front of her, bowing with respect. They did not raise their heads until Catalina touched them with her fleeting fingers and mechanically recited the salutation of courtesy.

When this ceremony was complete, they went on their way. Even though they all knew the road, not one dared to take a step without following the *ilol*. It was evident from their expectant, solicitous overtures that these women considered her a superior. Not out of respect for her husband's position, since all were wives of public officials and some of higher rank than Winikton, but because of the fame that transformed Catalina in the eyes of these unfortunate, fearful souls, so eager to ingratiate themselves with the supernatural.

Catalina allowed the veneration with the calm certainty of one receiving her due. The submission of the others made her neither uncomfortable nor vain. Her conduct was one of tactful but grudging response to the tribute paid her. Her reply was an approving smile, an understanding look, an opportune counsel, a fortuitous observation. And yet she always went armed with the threatening possibility of causing harm, though she herself was careful to keep her power in check. She had already seen how often the mighty had fallen.

And so, Catalina marched at the head of the procession of Tzotzil women, all uniformly dressed in thick, dark garments. All bent under the weight of their burdens (wares to sell, sleeping babies). All on their way to Ciudad Real.

The path, made by constant travel, wound around the hillsides. Loose, ocher earth, the kind that is easily swept away by the wind. Hostile vegetation. Weeds, twisted thorns. And all along the way, shrubs, bushes, peach trees dressed in their finery, smiling and glowing with happiness.

The distance between Saint John Chamula and Ciudad Real (or Jobel in the Indian language) is long. But these women could travel it without growing tired, without conversation. Attentive to where they placed their feet and to the labor of their hands, which produced wheels of woven threads that grew longer with each step.

The massive chain of mountains comes to rest in an extensive valley. Here and there, scattered as if allowed to fall carelessly, the houses appear. Tile-roofed buildings, dwellings of the Ladinos who tend their flocks and gardens, they offer precarious refuge from the weather. At times, with the insolence of its isolation, a hacienda comes into view. Strong and solid, its sinister appearance is more like that of a fortress than a dwelling for the idle rich.

Outlying areas, suburbs. From there one can see the towers of the churches, reflecting the light in the moisture-laden air.

Catalina Díaz Puiljá stopped and crossed herself. Her followers imitated her. And then, amid hurried whispers and skillful maneuverings, they redistributed the merchandise they were carrying. Some women took all they could carry. The others only pretended to bend under their heavy loads. These went on ahead.

Quietly, like those who neither see nor hear, who expect no sudden disturbance, the Tzotzil women went on their way.

When they turned the first corner, it happened—no less fearsome and repulsive for being expected or habitual. Five Ladino women from the lower class, barefoot and poorly dressed, attacked Catalina and her companions. Without a word of threat or insult, without explaining why, the Ladino women tried to snatch the nets of eggs, the clay pots, the cloth, from the hands of the Indian women, who defended themselves with brave and silent furor. But in the midst of the fight, both sides took care not to damage or break the disputed objects.

Taking advantage of the confusion of the first few moments, some of the Indian women were able to escape and ran into the center of Ciudad Real. Meanwhile those who remained behind opened their injured hands and surrendered their belongings to the attackers, who triumphantly took possession of the bounty. And to give their violence the appearance of legitimacy, they hurled a fistful of copper coins at the enemy, who knelt, weeping, and gathered them from the dust.

Translated by Myralyn F. Allgood

Editor's Note: This excerpt, from *Another Way to Be: Selected Works of Rosario Castellanos,* is the first chapter of the novel *Oficio de tinieblas.* Its title is taken, as the translator notes, "from the Tenebrae Service that is part of the celebration of Good Friday. It consists of gradually extinguishing the altar candles to signify the darkness that fell over the world after the crucifixion of Jesus Christ." First published in Spanish in 1962, the novel recounts an uprising of Maya Indians in Chiapas, set in the 1930s but inspired by actual uprisings in the eighteenth and nineteenth centuries.

Swift as Desire

Laura Esquivel

HE WAS BORN HAPPY and on a holiday. Welcomed into
the world by his whole family, gathered together for the
special day. They say his mother laughed so hard at one of
the jokes being told around the table that her waters broke.
At first she thought the dampness between her legs was
urine that she had not been able to contain because of her
laughter but she soon realized that this was not the case,
that the torrent was a signal that her twelfth child was
about to be born. Still laughing, she excused herself and
went to her bedroom. As she had gone through eleven
previous deliveries, this one took only a few minutes, and

LAURA ESQUIVEL (1951–) was born in Mexico City. Her
novel *Like Water for Chocolate* (1990), sold over four million
copies, was translated into thirty-five languages, and was made
into an award-winning movie based on her screenplay of the
same title. Her more recent novels are *The Law of Love* (1996)
and *Swift as Desire* (2001), from which this excerpt is taken. In
1993 she was named Mexico's Woman of the Year, and in 1994
she became the first foreigner to receive the American Book-
sellers Association Award. She divides her time between Mexico City and New York.

she gave birth to a beautiful boy who, instead of coming into the world crying, entered it laughing.

After bathing, Doña Jesusa returned to the dining room. "Look what happened to me!" she announced to her relatives. Everyone turned to look at her, and, revealing the tiny bundle she held in her arms, she said, "I laughed so hard, the baby came out."

A loud burst of laughter filled the dining room and everyone enthusiastically applauded the happy occasion. Her husband, Librado Chi, raised his arms and exclaimed, "*¡Qué júbilo!*"—"What joy!"

And that was what they named him. In truth, they could not have chosen a better name. Júbilo was a worthy representative of joy, of pleasure, of joviality. Even when he became blind, many years later, he always retained his sense of humor. It seemed as if he had been born with a special gift for happiness. And I don't mean simply a capacity for being happy, but also a talent for bringing happiness to everyone around him. Wherever he went, he was accompanied by a chorus of laughter. No matter how heavy the atmosphere, his arrival, as if by magic, would always ease tension, calm moods, and cause the most pessimistic person to see the brighter side of life, as if, above all else, he had the gift of bringing peace. The only person with whom this gift failed him was his wife, but that isolated case constituted the sole exception to the rule. In general, there was no one who could resist his charm and good humor. Even Itzel Ay, his paternal grandmother—the woman who, after her son had married a white woman, had been left with a permanent frown etched on her forehead—began to smile when she saw Júbilo. She called him Che'ehunche'eh Wich, which in the Mayan language means "the one with the smiling face."

The relationship between Doña Jesusa and Doña Itzel was far from good until after Júbilo was born. Because of race. Doña Itzel was one hundred percent Mayan Indian and she disapproved of the mixing of her race's blood with Doña Jesusa's Spanish blood. For many years, she had avoided visiting her son's home. Her grandchildren grew up without her being very involved in their lives. Her rejection of her daughter-in-law was so great that for years she refused to speak to her, arguing that she couldn't speak Spanish. So Doña Jesusa was forced to learn Mayan in order to be able to speak with her mother-in-law. But she found it very difficult to learn a new language while raising twelve children, so communication between the two was sparse and of poor quality.

But all that changed after Júbilo was born. As she desired with all her soul to be near the baby, his grandmother began to visit her son's house again, which had never happened with the other grandchildren, as if she had no great interest in them. But from the first moment she saw Júbilo, she became fascinated with his smiling face. Júbilo was a blessing to the family; he appeared like a gift from heaven that no one expected. A beautiful gift that they didn't know what to do with. The difference in age between him and the youngest of his siblings was several years, and a few of his older brothers and sisters were already married and had children of their own. So it was almost as if Júbilo were an only child, and his playmates were his nieces and nephews, who were the same age as he. Because his mother was busy simultaneously fulfilling the roles of mother, wife, grandmother, mother-in-law, and daughter-in-law, Júbilo spent a lot of time in the company of the servants, until his grandmother adopted him as her favorite grandchild. They spent most of the day together, taking walks, playing, talking. Of course, his grandmother spoke to him in Mayan, which meant that Júbilo became Doña Itzel's first bilingual grandchild. And so, from the age of five, the child became the family's official interpreter. This was a fairly complicated matter for a small child, as he had to take into account that when Doña Jesusa said the word *mar*, she was referring to the sea in front of their home, where the family often swam. On the other hand, when Doña Itzel said the word *K'ak'nab*, she wasn't referring only to the sea, but also to the "lady of the sea," which is the name given to one of the phases of the moon and is associated with large bodies of water. Both of these entities have the same name in Mayan. So, as Júbilo translated, not only did he have to be aware of these subtleties, but he also had to pay attention to his mother's and grandmother's tone of voice, the tension in their vocal cords, as well as the expressions on their faces and the set of their mouths. It was a difficult task, but one which Júbilo performed with great pleasure. Of course, he didn't always translate literally. He always added a kind word or two to soften the exchange between the two women. Over time, this little trick managed to help them get along a little better each day, and they eventually grew to love one another.

Translated by Stephen Lytle